THE CULTURE DRIVEN ORGANIZATION

How to Create Your Desired Organizational Culture and Sustain It

Eyad J. Mubaied

Copyright © 2024 by Cultivate Culture, LLC

All rights reserved.

No part of this publication may be reproduced, distributed, or transmitted in any form or by any means, including photocopying, recording, or other electronic or mechanical methods, without the prior written permission of the publisher, except as permitted by U.S. copyright law. For permission requests, contact: info@cultivateculturellc.com. For privacy reasons, some names, locations, and dates may have been changed.

Book Cover Design: Lou Morales
Cover image: © Shutterstock.com
Author portrait: Dean Stewart Photography, Inc.
Editor: Melinda Ronn
ISBN: 9798321999295

DEDICATION

To God,
the original Creator of culture.

TABLE OF CONTENTS

Introduction .... Pg. 1

Chapter One: What is Culture? .... Pg. 5

Chapter Two: The Secret Recipe....................................... Pg. 17

Chapter Three: Philosophy .... Pg. 23

Chapter Four: Process .... Pg. 51

Chapter Five: People .... Pg. 79

Chapter Six: Sustainment .... Pg. 93

Organizational Culture Assessment .... Pg. 102

Author Biography.. Pg. 104

Cultivate Culture LLC .... Pg. 105

INTRODUCTION

"You can't make this stuff up!"

I'm sure you have uttered that phrase more than once in your lifetime. Whether you have encountered situations that left you baffled or experienced extraordinary circumstances and peculiar behavior, there is no doubt that like you, we all encounter times in life when all we can do is exclaim, "You can't make this stuff up!"

My career journey began working as a temporary employee at State Street Bank in Boston, concurrently holding a night position as a sales representative at the local Radio Shack. Throughout my career, I have worked on different continents and with different organizations, representing many industries, large and small, for-profit and not-for-profit, small teams and large ones. I have witnessed countless cultures and encountered multitudes of interactions that made me think, "One day I should write a book." And here we are!

Culture is an essential element for the functioning of any organization. I observed many cultures, some were favorable, and others were not. According to a Deloitte survey, 94% of executives believe culture is essential but only 36% indicate the culture is aligned with the business strategy. Many leaders ignore the effects of culture or don't even know about the topic. It might be because they don't care or when they do, simply think it is too difficult or don't know how to create a good culture. Throughout my experiences, I discovered a simple, yet profound "secret recipe" to create and sustain a desired culture that I feel compelled to share with the world.

This book serves as a clarion call to leaders. It is my dream that this recipe will be applied to inspire multitudes, increase employee engagement, solidify vision and purpose, elevate your organization to function at its best, and result in a greater good for humanity.

Let me be clear—I've made numerous mistakes in my career and life, and many lessons have been learned in the process. I am far from perfect, as is any leader today, yesterday, or tomorrow. Yet, through the difficulties, the successful strategies, and the ones that fell short, I have seen great success come about when the recipe is followed.

Before we delve into the content, let me provide some key points to ensure you have the right expectations:

Focus On The "How"

Numerous books, articles, workshops, and courses have explored the concept of culture over the years, often delving into the ingredients necessary for a positive culture. They emphasize elements such as creating a sense of safety, fostering open and honest communication, and other vital components. This analogy likens building a good culture to preparing a dish—combining protein, salt, rice, veggies, etc., resulting in a desired outcome.

Similarly, discussions often touch upon the traits of leaders aiming to cultivate a positive culture. Leaders who are visionary, compassionate yet firm, creative, and those driven by data are likened to skilled cooks essential for achieving the desired cultural "dish."

However, this book takes a distinctive approach by primarily addressing the "how" question. Using the analogy of cooking, it serves as a recipe guide—outlining the steps and processes, such as when to add specific elements and how long to let them simmer. Unlike many resources, it places the spotlight on the procedural aspects rather than the ingredients or the cook, although these elements are acknowledged throughout the narrative.

Imperfect Yet Effective Recipe

The presented secret recipe is not flawless, but adhering to its principles enhances the likelihood of establishing the desired organizational culture in the most effective and efficient way. Flexibility in following it would still yield positive results.

Assumptions About Leadership

This book assumes organizational leaders believe in its principles, reflect them in actions, and aspire to create and sustain a particular desired culture. The culture you desire as a leader cannot be different than the culture you live out.

Good Leaders
Continuing in the same vein, it's important to note that leaders don't necessarily have to be labeled as "good" leaders. While this book is not explicitly focused on cultivating "good" culture, the aspiration is that its principles are harnessed to construct cultures considered beneficial and, ultimately, advantageous for humanity. However, in practical terms, the same principles outlined in this book are equally applicable when dealing with cultures that may not be considered positive. The universal nature of these principles allows for their effectiveness in both fostering favorable cultures and addressing challenges within less favorable ones.

Relevance To Various Roles
You don't need to be the Chief Executive Officer (CEO) or a president of the organization for this book to apply. It's relevant to leaders and managers at various levels, recognizing that each leader may impact a distinct culture within the organization.

Harmonizing Sub-Cultures
In larger organizations, following these principles at the top level increases the likelihood of consistent sub-cultures, minimizing conflicting or inconsistent pockets.

Impact On Every Individual
Whether you're a leader or not, you play a role in the organization's culture. Understanding and applying the principles in this book enables you to strategically influence or assess your fit within the culture.

Applicability Across Organizations
The principles outlined apply universally, whether to small or large companies, public or private entities, households, non-profits, faith-based organizations, or government entities.

Individual Application

Surprisingly, the same principles listed in this book apply to individuals. As an organism, you can use them to cultivate a desired personal culture, influencing your behavior and conduct.

Interchangeable Topics

While some topics align with specific chapters, you will notice that certain subjects are multi-layer and interchangeably discussed throughout the book (i.e. Philosophy, Process, or People).

Book Title

The title was crafted to assist leaders who intentionally want to create and sustain a desired culture in their organization. It's crucial to clarify that while this book doesn't explicitly delve into the impact of external cultural factors on organizations, there is a strong correlation, and these external factors can exert a significant influence. Consequently, the principles presented in this book serve as a valuable tool, helping leaders become cognizant of external cultural influences and empowering them to manage these effects in a way that aligns with their organizational goals—either welcoming or rejecting them as desired.

Privacy Considerations

While all stories shared are factual, please note that identities (including names, companies, and locations) are fictionalized to protect privacy unless specifically identified as real name.

Now, with all these intentions being said, let's begin our journey!

CHAPTER ONE
WHAT IS CULTURE?

"Culture is the arts of the mind"
—Thomas Carlyle

I distinctly recall my inaugural visit to In-N-Out Burger (real name). Throughout the entire experience, from entrance to exit, I was struck by the meticulous attention to detail, the consistently pleasant interactions, and the exceptional quality of the food. Yet, what left a lasting impression was the cohesive atmosphere. It reminded me of a finely tuned orchestra. Despite diverse roles, each team member performed their tasks with synchronicity, creating a harmony that elevated the overall experience, and made me return to In-N-Out repeatedly.

During a recent visit to a newly constructed Costco (real name), I encountered a similar experience. The thorough arrangement of products, transparent pricing, positive interactions with the staff, and the overall cleanliness of the warehouse left, yet again, an enduring impression on me. Every aspect of their methodology and team contributed to a seamless and satisfying shopping environment.

What these organizations shared resulted in a positive impact on me as their customer and made me want to return to their establishment. They both had "good cultures."

WHAT IS CULTURE?

Culture can have many definitions. The word "culture" derives from a French term, which in turn derives from the Latin "colere," which means to tend to and grow, or cultivate and nurture. It's related to actively fostering growth.

The Merriam Webster Dictionary defines it as "the customary beliefs, social norms, and material traits of a racial, religious, or social group" or "the characteristic features of everyday existence (such as diversions or a way of life) shared by people in a place or time."

Wikipedia defines culture as "a concept that encompasses the social behavior, institutions, and norms found in human societies, as well as the knowledge, beliefs, arts, laws, customs, capabilities, and habits of the individuals in these groups. Culture is often originated from or attributed to a specific region or location."

Growing up in the Middle East, I learned a cultural norm that when invited to someone's home for lunch (the main meal of the day), it is customary for the host to immediately add more food to your plate once you have finished your first serving. If you refuse the second serving, it is considered impolite. This practice is deeply rooted in the cultural fabric, emphasizing the significance of hospitality and respect.

Likewise, when considering Japanese culture, bowing is a significant aspect of human interactions, taking on many different expressions. At times it's a gesture employed when greeting others, showing respect, or even offering apologies. Even the depth and angle of the bow can convey different meanings based on the context. This practice is deeply ingrained in the culture, highlighting how cultural values shape human relations and communication norms.

In various regions, cultural norms differ significantly. For instance, in some parts of the world, it's considered disrespectful for kids to make direct eye contact with their elders during a conversation. Conversely, in other cultures, avoiding direct eye contact can be viewed as rude. The variations in these practices underscore the influence of cultural values and customs on interpersonal interactions.

In certain countries, it's inappropriate to disagree with elders, while in others, expressing dissent is not only acceptable but expected. Similarly, cultural nuances dictate that putting your hands in your pockets during a conversation may be frowned upon in some cultures but inconsequential in others.

At one point in my career, I worked with a subsidiary of a large German company. During an involved and far-reaching project, I had to travel to Germany to meet with the primary leadership team. While there, we engaged in numerous work sessions, interspersed with breaks where discussions covered a variety of topics, including the project at hand.

One evening, as we worked past sunset, I noticed that no one bothered to turn on the lights in the conference room, and it wasn't due to a motion detector malfunction. Initially, I thought it was merely a product of everyone's intense focus, but when I asked one of my German colleagues about it later, I discovered the real reason. During the blackouts of World War II, the Germans became accustomed to working in the dark. Though the war was long over, this habit became ingrained in the culture as a lasting legacy from the past.

I could continue sharing various stories about cultural traits, but the fundamental questions remain. How were these traits taught? Who initiated them? How did they transcend generations? Were they part of citizenship tests or explicitly taught in schools? In certain cases, the answers are clear. In many others, the origins remain obscure. For some, it's as straightforward as the Mandalorians proclaiming, "This is the Way."

In my experience, when posing this question on how to define culture to an organization—whether it's a company, a group of people, your household, or even yourself—I define culture as "the manifestation of the shared beliefs reflected in common behaviors."

Applying the above concept to the corporate workplace or any organization, the question arises: What is their "culture"? Do they indeed have a discernible culture? Can the absence of a consistent culture be considered a type of culture in and of itself?

GOOD VS. BAD? RIGHT VS. WRONG?

It's crucial to emphasize, especially in the context of people and societal cultures, that this is not a question of good or bad; right or wrong. Cultural traits, encompassing beliefs and behaviors, simply exist as they are.

The same principle applies to organizational culture. It's not about categorizing it as good or bad, and right or wrong. Organizations can have diverse culture traits, ranging from a 'results-driven' focus to an emphasis on the process that leads to results. Some may adopt a 'command and control' culture, while others lean towards a 'servant leadership' approach. The usefulness of each may vary based on factors such as time, place, and circumstances. The choice often becomes a matter of preference or a deliberate leadership decision aiming for a more efficient and effective method of achieving organizational goals.

WHAT ARE THE RESULTS OF CULTURE?

According to a Gallup study conducted in 2020, disengaged employees have 37% higher absenteeism, 18% lower productivity, and 15% lower profitability. When that translates into dollars, it costs 34% of a disengaged employee's annual salary or $3,400 for every $10,000 they make. The opposite is true for engaged employees. Per a Harvard Business Review survey, an organization with a strong culture of innovation is 3.5 times more likely to out-perform its peers in revenue growth.

The level of employee engagement or disengagement is often the reflection of various culture traits within an organization. These in turn significantly influence the overall employee experience and commitment, which plays a pivotal role in shaping the broader stakeholder experience, including the customers, or served group.

When I began drafting this book in early 2024, there was a noteworthy incident involving Costco (real name). In December 2023, certain Costco employees at a specific location voted to unionize, expressing their intention to enhance working conditions at the wholesale retail chain. Specifically, the workers aimed for a union, such as the Teamsters, to advocate for higher wages, pension contributions, bonuses, and a more flexible attendance policy, among other improvements. Costco responded to the event through a press release, stating, "The fact that a majority of the location's employees felt that they wanted or needed a union constitutes a failure on our part."

Setting aside any personal stance on unions or beliefs in employee rights, the tone of Costco's press release is indicative of a specific culture that the leaders at Costco intended or currently aim to foster. This same culture is a fundamental factor behind the remarkable almost doubling of Costco's stock price in the brief span from 2021 to 2024. While stock price alone is not the sole measure of a company's success, it does reflect a certain culture, particularly when assessing long-term results.

On one particular occasion, after undergoing a 360 Feedback Survey to assess my leadership style, I engaged in a discussion about the results with my Human Resources (HR) representative. While our conversation initially centered around the survey, it naturally evolved into a broader exploration of organizational culture.

The conversation went something like this:

HR: Eyad, take me as an example. It's been my tendency to respond promptly to any question I know the answer to. However, during a recent conversation with my supervisor, he advised against this approach

Eyad: Oh really, what did he say?

HR: He suggested that instead of providing an immediate response, I should communicate to the person that I'll investigate the question, take a couple of days, and then return with the answer.

Eyad: Oh, that's interesting. So even if you know the answer you would take two days and then get back to them?

HR: Yes, the intention behind this approach is to convey an open-minded and thorough consideration of the question. Taking the time to research and return with a well-considered and accurate response can enhance the perception of thoughtfulness and expertise.

Eyad (after pausing for a few seconds): Interesting. Let's say I am the one asking you for the answer, if I knew that you knew the answer but took two days to deliver it, couldn't that lead me to believe that you just wasted two days' worth of time?

The conversation illuminated the type of culture within HR and the broader company culture. If the CEO discovered that the standard practice involved a two-day delay in responses to avoid being perceived as "close-minded," and resulting in upsetting an important person, would that be acceptable or align with the desired culture and results?

The impact on operational results and goal achievement might vary based on the desired culture. While the above particular behavior may not directly correlate with employee satisfaction or engagement, it could influence the overall efficiency and functioning of the organization.

WHAT CULTURE EXISTS IN YOUR ORGANIZATION?

There are many organizational culture types, each with distinctive traits, which can be organized and categorized in various ways. Here are a few concepts to consider:

1. **Your process:** Is it fully automated vs. manual, highest-integrity vs. legal-focused, role-based vs. task-oriented, centralized decision-making vs. decentralized, or documented vs. spoken? This category is intricately linked to the desired character of the organization's processes.

2. **Your team:** Would you define it as collaborative vs. consensus vs. command and control, problem-focused vs. opportunity-focused, task-focused vs. relationship-focused, service-oriented vs. results-oriented, control conscientious vs. risk and opportunity conscientious, formal vs. informal, form driven vs. substance driven, profit focus vs. social focus, or factual vs. feeling/spirited? This category pertains to the behaviors exhibited by the team, focusing on internal dynamics among team members or how they engage with external stakeholders.

3. **Your stakeholder:** This category is defined through the lens of the stakeholders your organization serves. Whether they are customers, vendors, financial institutions, community members, etc., consider the

impact you want to have on your stakeholders—do they consider you fair vs. shrewd, customer-first vs. sale first, short-term vs. long-term relationship, service-driven vs. purpose-driven?

There are many ways you can categorize and characterize culture traits. It's unrealistic to encapsulate it with just one word or a singular character, given the multifaceted nature of cultural dynamics. Further, the above trait opposites are not necessarily concluded as favorable vs. unfavorable since the selection of the trait might need to be based on the desired outcome.

LOOK CLOSER, WHAT DO YOU NOTICE?

Many culture traits are not immediately evident and may require careful observation and consideration to uncover. In some instances, these traits become apparent only through the outcomes or results they produce. The subtlety of these cultural aspects can make them more challenging to identify, but understanding their impact on results is key to deciphering them.

William's Story

William found himself working at a company that experienced significant changes. In fact, when he joined the corporate team, he was promptly informed that he had a three-month window to implement changes, as failure to do so would position him as part of the problem. While William recognized, and in part agreed with this philosophy, he didn't fully anticipate the challenges and the toll it would take to institute the changes the company had hired him to make.

From the outset, William began to observe certain phenomena, though the significance of these observations only became clear several years later.

For instance, during his interview process, the job description bore a certain title that wasn't equal to his peers who reported to the same supervisor. On William's very first day, as he walked with his supervisor from one building to another, the supervisor conveyed to William that HR mentioned he couldn't use his title in company interactions, including in his email signature!

You can imagine how surprised William was at his supervisor's directive from HR. Though he accepted what his supervisor said, he also politely asked if he could know "why" HR gave that directive. It was by all means a legitimate question.

The supervisor explained to William that they didn't want to offend other direct reports since he was the only one with that specific title.

As odd as that sounded to William, he told his supervisor he didn't care about the title but rather his scope and authority. Interestingly enough, the supervisor acquiesced and told William he could use his title, including on his emails, but not to add any other emphasis to it. The conversation ended with William's supervisor suggesting that he should not listen to HR.

William reiterated his perspective, stating that it was not a big deal and that he would move forward without dwelling on the title matter.

Upon hearing William's story, the interaction indeed seems peculiar. One might wonder if HR had been involved in finalizing the job description. If William's role were genuinely expressed through the title, why would HR have concerns about the potential feelings of others since the scope of William's work differed? Ideally, these matters should have been clarified before William's start date. Moreover, the supervisor is typically the one who makes the final decision as to an employee's title. The entire situation raises questions about the clarity and communication within the organization's processes and culture at large.

William encountered another interaction with HR when his team sought to hire a lower-level employee in his department. Following standard procedure, his team created a job description, engaged his HR Partner to ensure a clear understanding of the requirements, and went through the customary hiring processes.

The interviewing process commenced, and there was a particular candidate that William's team wanted to assess through interviews. This individual seemed to possess the skills deemed necessary, at least on paper.

HR was slated to conduct the initial interview, followed by the rest of

William's team. However, after the HR interview was completed, an abrupt cancellation for all subsequent interviews was sent to the team without any explanation or conversation. About a week later, during a call with HR, William's team inquired about the sudden cancellation. HR then revealed that during their interview, the candidate had made statements that were not in alignment with company values.

The abrupt cancellation was disappointing for William's team, especially considering their positive impression of the candidate. This raised questions for William. "Why did HR cancel the interviews without informing us? Why didn't they feel the need to consult with us first or strongly recommend canceling the interviews, with the option to escalate if we disagreed? Isn't HR supposed to serve us as a function? In this scenario, who is the customer, and who is the service provider? Would a service provider typically cancel their service or implement such changes without customer input?"

Irrespective of whether the behavior shown in both stories was right or wrong, it left William with the perception that HR held significant influence within the company. Subsequently, he found that to make progress within the organization, appeasing HR was a crucial factor.

Over time, as William continued his tenure at the company, he began questioning why the culture prioritized HR over other functions. It came to his attention that the CEO's closest confidant was none other than the head of HR. The head of HR held a unique position where no one dared to disagree, criticize, or challenge the CEO—except, interestingly enough, the head of HR.

Since the CEO brought in the head of HR from his previous company, it was a clear signal to others of the CEO's high regard for HR. This close relationship bestowed significant power upon HR, regardless of complaints from various departments. The unique bond between the head of HR and the CEO fostered a culture where HR held substantial influence and, in many ways, ruled the organization.

One of my colleagues told me a story about a team where the supervisor unconsciously favored one individual, which created a culture where that person became the de facto representative for the team in discussions or negotiations with the supervisor. This dynamic, though possibly unintentional, significantly influenced the team's culture and impacted the decision-making process, thereby affecting the team's overall goals and objectives, either directly or indirectly.

SWIMMING UPSTREAM?

Implementing cultural changes within an organization, especially in larger settings, can be a challenging assignment. The ease of making such changes depends on factors like the presence and extent of the existing culture, as well as the strategy, consensus, or directives from executive leaders to bring about the desired cultural creation or cultural shift.

A unified tone among top leadership significantly enhances the likelihood of a thriving culture. While it's not essential for the CEO or executive leadership to align on every specific aspect of culture, following the secret recipe [to be discussed in Chapter 2] can boost the chances of success across different parts of the organization. However, having senior leaders on the same page exponentially reduces the time and effort needed to create and/or sustain the desired culture.

Aleksandr's Story

Upon joining a well-known company and becoming a part of the Corporate team, Aleksandr swiftly discerned that there was an issue with the culture; specifically, as it related to who owns the responsibility of internal controls over financial reporting. This realization dawned on Aleksandr through various conversations, interactions, and the outcomes of day-to-day activities. The responsibility for internal controls was often attributed to the internal audit team or, in certain instances, the external audit team, although this wasn't explicitly documented or acknowledged. Aleksandr knew the culture was immature since a company of its size and nature would normally attribute the ownership to all process owners throughout the organization.

While Aleksandr's immediate supervisor appreciated his efforts to shift the culture towards process owners who would take ownership of internal controls, not all leaders were aligned. The leaders who embraced Aleksandr's perspective [and understood the rationale behind process owners owning internal controls] experienced positive outcomes. However, those who resisted caused numerous challenges to Aleksandr's team. Conversations were prolonged, efforts were more time-consuming, and navigating political battles became a frequent necessity.

In a pivotal meeting attended by the company CFO and all his direct reports, including various executives, Aleksandr presented the significant internal control initiatives that his team was leading. He emphasized the importance of collective alignment. However, one segment CFO, who was not a staunch supporter of Aleksandr –or his team's work due to the belief that the segment CFO didn't own internal controls –was resisting the team's efforts in a business unit undergoing a system implementation.

In the ongoing system implementation, Aleksandr's team was assisting the segment CFO's team in documenting the current process, which not only aided comprehension but also helped in facilitating the transition to the new system. However, the segment CFO dismissed this effort as futile, claiming that all documentation would be discarded post-implementation. Ironically, another division under his leadership, having undergone a similar implementation the previous year, faced post-implementation challenges, partially due to a lack of comprehensive understanding and documentation of the pre-and post-implementation process, risks, and controls.

Aleksandr addressed the segment CFO's concerns, emphasizing that the documentation efforts were strategic and not merely checkbox activities, aimed at ensuring a smooth implementation. Despite this clarification, the segment CFO continued to resist, requiring intervention from the company's CFO to compel him to move forward. Nonetheless, the political culture within the segment persisted, influencing priorities, and hindering collaboration with Aleksandr's team for an extended period.

CONCLUSION

Culture can play a pivotal role in the success or downfall of an organization. Its intangible nature is comparable to the wind—unseen but profoundly felt, shaping the outcomes and experiences within. Yet far too many organizations often overlook the importance of their culture.

In the next chapter, we will explore how to systematically create the desired culture for your organization.

QUESTIONS TO PONDER

1. Do you acknowledge the existence and significance of organizational culture?

2. Are you convinced that culture plays a crucial role in shaping your organization?

3. As the leader of your organization, do you recognize your responsibility for cultivating the culture within it?

4. Have you identified the prevailing culture in your organization? Have you invested time and effort into understanding it? Is that something you aspire to do?

5. Do you endorse or agree with the current organizational culture?

6. In cases where you find yourself at odds with the existing culture, what initiative-taking steps are you willing to take to transform it into a desired one? Is this a goal you are committed to achieving?

7. Considering the size of your organization, is there alignment across different hierarchical levels regarding the perceived culture, as envisioned by you (or others who are) the ultimate leader?

CHAPTER TWO
THE SECRET RECIPE

"Everything should be made as simple as possible, but not simpler"
—Albert Einstein

Throughout my 24 years of professional experience, I've observed various organizational cultures that have spanned corporate settings, faith-based environments, and within my own household. I have delved into books, engaged with diverse teams, listened to podcasts, and absorbed insights from keynote speakers. Through it all, I noticed a recurring pattern in the success or challenges of culture creation (distinct from the success or challenges of the culture itself, or the traits of the leader or leaders). It became noticeably clear that the presence of specific ingredients, as well as adherence to a systematic progression, led to thriving desired cultures. Conversely, in instances of challenges and issues, a deviation from either the essential ingredients or the prescribed process became apparent.

This is what I call the "Secret Recipe." When followed, the results were immensely successful. At one of the organizations I worked with, we shared these principles company-wide, particularly with those who harbored a passion for the subject and witnessed their subsequent success. The outcomes were so remarkable that some labeled them as miraculous, and individuals even received internal awards for the cultures they cultivated.

THE CULTURE CREATION MODEL

Creating your desired culture is simple. Choose a Philosophy (mindset or principles), integrate it into a Process (system, platform, or partnerships), and instill it in People (employees, members, or participants). When these three elements align, you have a path to creating the desired culture.

Here is a picture to illustrate the Model.

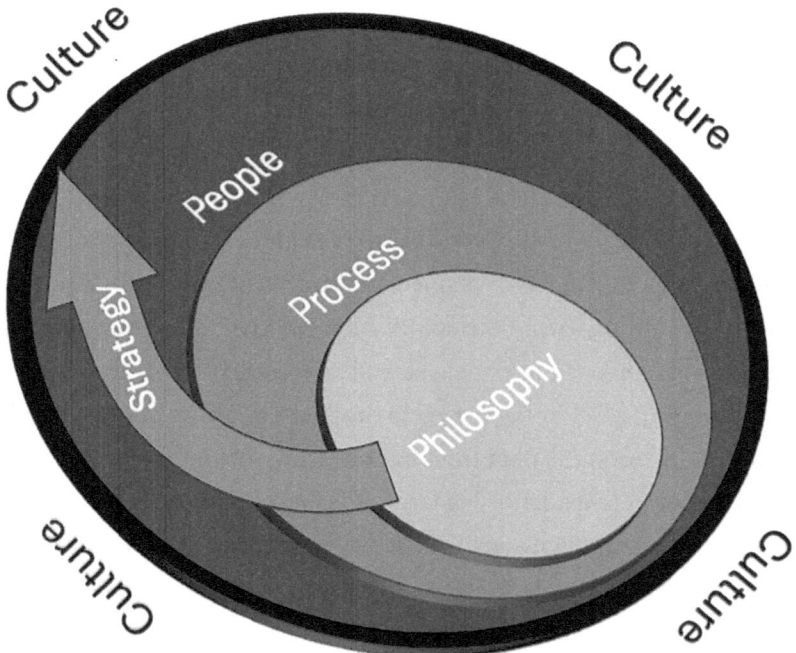

Figure 1: The Culture Creation Model

Culture creation is a goal that involves many challenges—budgets, people, customers, community. While applying the Secret Recipe does not guarantee your desired culture, your chances of success are much greater.

It's important to note that when the three elements—Philosophy, Process, and People—don't align, you still end up with a culture, though it might be confused, non-unified, or unintended. The key distinction is that it's not the desired culture.

Let's say that one thing essential to your organization is the adherence to having the "highest ethical standards" in everything you do. The question that follows is how do you integrate that into your Process? Do you just talk about it and expect everyone (People) to follow it? In other words, what strategy will you have to make sure People follow it? Do you instill it in your policies? Do you define what it means, then systematically and recurringly communicate it? Do you have an ethics hot line where employees can call when policies are violated? Do you survey employees about it annually? Do you act on it when there is sufficient evidence of violations?

In another example, let's say that the one thing essential to your organization is choosing a "servant leadership" culture over "command and control" culture. The question that follows is how do you integrate "servant leadership" into your Process? Do you just talk about it and expect everyone (People) to follow it? What strategy will you have to make sure People follow it? Do you instill it in your policies? Do you define what it means, then systematically and recurringly communicate it? Do you include it in your goals? Do you include it in your Human Resource processes such as hiring, firing, promotion, or demotion practices? Do you survey employees about it annually? Do you act on it when there is sufficient evidence of violations? Do you have specific training at the management level to promote servant leadership?

Many organizations assume that if leaders have the Philosophy and live it (a required element to create the desired culture) the culture will automatically be created because of the leader's belief. Many leaders and organizations jump to conclusions that when something is not working, the issue must be People. Sometimes, more mature leaders look beyond that and dig into the Process to see if that is causing the issue. But rarely, per my observation, do leaders dig deeper and assess whether the issue is stemming from their Philosophy. This model will help you take systematic steps to create the desired culture. Conversely, when the results are not as expected, it will help you assess and identify the root cause.

Additionally, external factors or cultures surrounding the organization may try to influence or impact your organizational culture. The strength of your internal culture, shaped by following the Secret Recipe, will determine how your People, including leaders, respond to these external influences.

STRATEGY VS. CULTURE

After years of crystallizing this Secret Recipe with my various teams, we continued to use it in the same fashion in different organizations and capacities. We strategically put it in manuals, training materials, meetings, and speeches. In every case, it helped focus the efforts of leadership and organizational teams throughout the companies that used the recipe to create the desired culture.

Numerous studies conducted over the years consistently indicate that building a robust organizational culture can span a period of 3-5 years. However, the exact timeframe can be influenced by variables like the organization's size, location, and composition. Achieving this timeline necessitates strategic and intentional efforts from leaders and the organization. Without a prioritized and strategic approach, the process may extend beyond the suggested timeline or, in some cases, might not materialize at all. Jeff Bezos, the founder and CEO of Amazon, used to put an empty chair at each meeting, representing the customer. This ensured that the Amazon culture kept the customer front and center in their minds.

You've likely read or heard Peter Drucker's famous quote, "Culture eats strategy for breakfast." I wholeheartedly agree that Culture surpasses Strategy in importance, especially in achieving results and fostering a cohesive work environment. However, crafting a desired culture cannot be a random process, especially when trying to achieve it within a 3–5-year period. In the Secret Recipe, strategy plays a crucial role in every stage of the process. Strategic considerations are essential—before, during, and after the establishment of every aspect of the culture.

Layla's Story

Layla was employed at a company that experienced substantial growth through acquisitions. The first acquisition resulted in a 50% expansion, and a few years later, another merger led to 100% growth. While Layla wasn't privy to the inner workings of top senior executive management, she engaged with individuals who were. Observing the changes in the company's culture during the two major acquisitions was enlightening for Layla.

In the initial acquisition, the CEO adopted a strategy of appointing an equal number of presidents from both the acquiring and acquired companies to form segments, assigning one president to each segment. This approach was replicated after the subsequent merger, maintaining a balanced representation with half the presidents originating from each side.

Layla pondered whether the CEO aimed to create a unified company culture from the two transactions. However, in practice, the company ended up with distinct subcultures, influenced by the leaders of each segment.

Inquiring with individuals engaged in the integration process, both internally and externally, Layla discovered that "culture" was not a clearly defined, separate, or distinct integration stream. This absence might have been a prominent contributing factor to the emergence of distinct sub-cultures within the company.

CONCLUSION

Utilizing the Secret Recipe of Philosophy, Process, and People empowers you to create a permeating, consistent, and enduring desired culture. Your perspective will shift from a micro-level to a macro-level view of your organization. You'll discern connections that were previously unseen, often highlighting the need for Philosophy changes as opposed to other elements. When this process is purposeful, it will ensure a more efficient and effective transformation.

In the next chapter, we will discuss and unpack Philosophy. This is where the first step of the process starts. Like the human body, action (critical to life) starts with the mind (or Philosophy). Once you define that, the path is much clearer; albeit filled with challenges!

Let's dig into Philosophy!

QUESTIONS TO PONDER

1. Is creating the desired culture a strategic process, or do you think it happens haphazardly?

2. At a broad level, do you understand the fundamental ingredients and steps, the Secret Recipe, required to establish the desired culture within your organization?

3. When you notice disparities in your organizational culture—whether it's not aligning with your organizational goals or being inconsistently applied—what actions do you take?

4. In situations where results are not achieved or there are breakdowns in Processes or People, do you immediately address the symptoms, or do you investigate the root cause, considering whether it's a Philosophy issue?

5. When everything is running smoothly, do you take the time to reflect on why it's successful? How do you ensure the continued success of your processes and culture?

CHAPTER THREE
PHILOSOPHY

"Philosophy is the highest music"
—Plato

To lay the groundwork for the desired culture, the initial step involves choosing a Philosophy that serves as the driving force of that culture. An alternative term for Philosophy is mindset. No matter which term you use, this element is the soul of culture. And similar to the human soul, this Philosophy may not be visible, yet it defines the essence and breathes life into the organizational body.

PHILOSOPHY IS THE SOUL OF CULTURE

Initiating the creation or transformation of culture involves posing questions that unveil, clarify, and outline the Philosophy or mindset. What resides in our minds? How do we perceive the principles, concepts, or beliefs?

Philosophy can be applied comprehensively within an organization, operating at both macro and micro levels. At the macro level, it defines the overarching purpose and existence of the organization. Simultaneously, at the micro level, it delineates the purpose of individual functions, aligning them with the broader organizational identity and goals. This top-down approach ensures that each function contributes to the overall purpose and success of the organization.

The Costco example in Chapter 1 illustrates the impact of Philosophy on organizational culture. The leaders at Costco fostered a Philosophy centered around open and honest communication and prioritizing employee concerns. This approach aimed to create an environment where employees felt free to express their expectations, reducing the need for unionization.

Mariam's Story

Mariam, chosen to spearhead a unified Finance function after a merger, was engaged in a conversation with Phil, her direct report from the other merged company, during a team event. As they walked downtown after dinner, Mariam shared her vision for the function and the direction she intended to lead the combined company in terms of their newly integrated function.

Mariam discussed her beliefs, about the Philosophy of employees owning their process documentation, with Phil. They delved into the practical aspects, specifically focusing on the use of flowcharts as a method of documenting processes, commonly known as "spaghetti charts" due to their complexity. Phil, however, let Mariam know that the company doesn't use flow charts since the regulators don't mandate them.

Phil's statement provided Mariam with valuable insights regarding the mindset of the leaders on that side of the merged company. It indicated that, according to their perspective, compliance was viewed as a mere requirement, a "check-the-box" Philosophy. Instead of contemplating what the divisions should do, the focus was on fulfilling what was deemed as "required."

In Chapter 1, we heard William's story about the interaction with his HR department who restricted usage of his title along with abruptly cancelling the interview process. The Philosophy was centered around HR's mindset of being an equal or controlling partner rather than a service provider. This is evident in the term "HR Partner," which might imply equality, but the dynamics reveal the opposite of a service provider relationship. The subtle Philosophy difference influences the design of Processes and subsequently shapes the overall organizational culture through its impact on People.

Similarly, posing Philosophy questions within specific functions, processes, or transactions aids in alignment. The greater the cohesion in these Philosophies, the more pronounced the impact across all facets of the organization—extending from the highest echelons to individual transactions and interactions.

Below are some highly recommended Philosophies that you might want to adopt in order to create your desired organizational culture.

VISION, MISSION, AND VALUES

Vision, Mission, and Values individually serve a purpose in articulating organizational Philosophy. Let's explore each term separately.

VISION

The proverb "Where there is no vision, the people perish," underscores the crucial role of vision in guiding a collective purpose. Vision, often described as "the ability to think about or plan the future with imagination or wisdom," is focused on the long-term future. It may represent an aspirational goal that might never be fully attained but serves as a persistent purpose that guides ongoing efforts and endeavors.

A Vision statement serves as the embodiment of an organization's purpose, expressing why it exists. Crafting a compelling vision statement involves considering the following points:

- **Endless:** A powerful vision statement is one that, to some extent, remains an ongoing pursuit. The organization continually strives to achieve it by consistently enhancing strategies to reach the goal. Acknowledging that the vision may never be fully realized, the focus lies on continuous improvement and persistent efforts.

    The Hunger Project, a renowned organization, encapsulates its vision in the statement '*a world without hunger.*' Recognizing the perpetual nature of this goal, the organization commits to tireless efforts until hunger is eradicated, embodying the spirit of an enduring pursuit. Best Buy articulates its vision with the statement, 'To positively impact the world, enrich people's lives through technology and contribute to the common good.' Embracing the idea of continuous progress, this vision serves as an enduring aspiration, recognizing the ongoing commitment to making a positive difference.

It's important to clarify that the suggestion is not to set unattainable goals. Instead, the emphasis is on establishing long-term objectives that define the essence of the organization and its enduring vision. These are goals that inherently require sustained effort and time for accomplishment.

- **Inspirational:** Inspiration is a key quality of a well-crafted vision statement. It should effectively inspire and motivate its members. Both of the previously mentioned vision statements are indeed inspirational. Ending hunger is a universal aspiration, and the vision of positively impacting the world and enriching lives through technology is inherently motivational.

- **Outwardly focused:** An effective vision statement is outwardly focused, centering on the customer or the 'served group.' In the case of The Hunger Project, the focus is on the world and the goal of solving hunger. Similarly, Best Buy's vision is outwardly focused, targeting the world, people, and the common good.

    Contrast the above with Boeing's (real name) vision statement, which says, "People working together as a global enterprise for aerospace industry leadership." Notice the lack of outward focus? The statement implies that Boeing's primary purpose is for people, both internally and externally, to collaborate and make the company a leader in the aerospace industry. However, it does not emphasize the impact or service to the recipient, falling short in terms of being outwardly focused.

I collaborated with a company that underwent significant growth within a short period. Prior to a major transaction, the company had an internal slogan that resembled a vision statement. Surprisingly, after the substantial transaction took place, the once-prominent slogan was no longer in circulation. I interacted with a segment CFO who had recently joined the organization and inquired about their vision statement. He responded by saying that the corporate CFO would say "it's to use our size for good." But in reality, he confessed that they did not have an official vision statement. That troubled both of us. After all, how do you inspire core employees to work hard to create the next new thing, with no vision or vision statement? How do you inspire the accountant who is working long hours to close the books? When employees ask "Who are we? What am I (the employee) and other employees here for?" the company needs to have an answer. And that answer is an endless, inspirational, and outwardly focused Vision statement.

MISSION

A Mission statement provides a shorter-term perspective by articulating specific goals in order to achieve a long-term vision. It's likened to a mission in a battle, representing the immediate objectives within the broader context of a war. In simpler terms, it answers the question: What are you aiming to accomplish in the next few years (Mission) to reach your long-term end goal (Vision)?

Using the Hunger Project as an example, their Mission statement is "to facilitate individual and collective action to transform the systems of inequity that create hunger and cause it to persist." This Mission serves as a guide for their actions in the short and medium-term, helping them work towards their long-term vision.

While a Mission statement may adapt to current internal and external factors, a Vision statement should remain unchanged unless there is a fundamental shift in the core identity and purpose of the organization.

VALUES

If the Vision represents the purpose or "why" of the organization, the Mission reflects the "what" for the next few years, then the Values embody the "how." Values are often principle-based and tend to remain consistent, encompassing attributes such as customer focus, excellence, quality, teamwork, integrity, and more.

In many societies, there is a tendency to be captivated by an individual's actions and their societal status, such as position, job, and wealth. This emphasis on end results often leads to idolizing the "stars." The focus tends to be on what people "do" and "who" they are, while the process of achieving these results, the "how," is often overlooked as long as the desired outcomes are achieved.

In organizations, Values play a crucial role in determining the "how" of achieving goals. While the focus may often be on visible actions and outcomes, Values provide the guiding principles for how the organization conducts itself in the process of pursuing its Vision and Mission.

Values function as the compass for leaders and individuals, influencing the approach they take to achieve their goals and navigate their professional and personal journeys. They shape the decision-making process, and the actions leaders undertake to attain their objectives.

Organizational Values serve as the collective compass for individuals within the organization, driving their behaviors, decisions, and interactions. In successful organizations, a strong emphasis on these Values contributes to a positive and cohesive culture.

Like societies, organizations often have a multitude of Values, but they typically identify the most critical ones as "Core Values." In the following sections of this chapter, we will delve into some of these core values, as well as the guiding principles and Philosophies that influence them.

CORE VALUES

Integrity, The Core Of All Core Values

In my perspective, integrity stands at the core of all core values. Why? Because integrity serves as the root to the branches. While every aspect of a tree is essential, the branches can't bear fruit without a root that nourishes everything else.

Integrity is the foundation that enables you to be a valuable and respectful team member, provide excellent customer service, create outstanding products, and treat everyone with respect and without discrimination.

When faced with the dilemma of another core value conflicting with integrity, which one will be prioritized? For example, let's say that customer satisfaction conflicts with integrity. In the given example, the option that upholds integrity should take priority, even if it means the customer goal is not immediately achieved. This decision ensures long-term trust in the organization's actions.

In the early 2000s, during my time at KPMG (real name), I vividly remember the repercussions of Enron's collapse, which resulted in the demise of Arthur Andersen, one of the leading "Big 5" CPA firms of that period.

KPMG also faced a scandal involving tax shelters. Before this incident, KPMG adhered to the typical core values such as customer focus, excellence, teamwork, respect, and integrity, among others. There were seven values, the last one specifically addressed integrity, stating, "We act with integrity."

Following the tax shelter incident, which posed a significant threat to KPMG's existence, the organization underwent a comprehensive reevaluation of its core values. The severity of the situation prompted KPMG to scrutinize and reassess its guiding principles.

I distinctly recall that KPMG, in response to the tax shelter incident, unveiled updated core values. While the seven core values largely remained unchanged, a subtle yet significant modification was made to the "integrity" core value. The revised version read, "Above all, we act with integrity." This slight alteration carried considerable importance, and here's the rationale behind it.

KPMG recognized that, in critical situations, their commitment was to "above all" act with integrity. The adjustment to this core value signified that had this principle been prioritized during the tax shelter incident, it could have led to different decisions, potentially saving the company from the challenges it faced in subsequent years.

Ahmad's Story

Ahmad was employed at a company where the Chief Accounting Officer

(CAO) held quarterly meetings before the end of each quarter. These sessions were attended by all controllership and accounting employees, which featured guest speakers, updates, and pertinent information related to the ongoing quarter.

During one such meeting, the CAO extended an invitation to a segment CFO who provided an update on the segment's performance. Following the segment CFO's presentation, the floor was opened for questions, and the CAO posed a thoughtful and fair inquiry to the segment CFO. The CAO asked, "Ali, considering you are one of our customers, what are your expectations regarding the service we provide? How can we enhance our service to better meet your needs?"

Keep in mind that given the CAO's responsibility for accounting policy, segments often sought guidance from the Accounting organization on accounting-related matters.

In response, the segment CFO promptly expressed, "It would be greatly beneficial for the Accounting team to recognize that when we approach you with accounting queries, you must bear in mind the collective interest of our organization, and we require responses that align with the best interests of the company."

For the typical employee present, this response might have seemed acceptable, and one could argue its appropriateness and accuracy. However, this reply gave Ahmad a pause. He pondered whether, in the segment CFO's perspective, the correctness or incorrectness of the accounting answer mattered. Did it matter if they violated a policy or breached public trust? It appeared clear in the segment CFO's mind that they required an answer for the "good of the company," and as long as that objective was met, other values would take a backseat.

If a core value places the company above all else, and it conflicts with another core value like integrity, in that particular mindset or Philosophy, the company takes precedence. Applying the same principles, could the actions or inactions at Enron (real name) before its collapse be justified? Could they have argued that their actions were "for the good of the shareholders"?

Highest Ethical Standards

When a new CFO at one of the companies I worked with emphasized "Highest Ethical Standards" as a top priority, it raised a thought-provoking question: does this imply the existence of multiple levels of integrity? This was a concept that had not occurred to me before. While I had always perceived things as either ethical or not, the term "highest ethical standards" brought forth a new perspective.

When considering the possibility of multiple levels of integrity—ranging from the lowest being "legal," then a higher level termed "acceptable integrity," and finally the top one denoted as "highest integrity"—the crucial question arises: why opt for the highest standard? Why not settle for the lower or medium levels? This prompts a deeper exploration into why organizations should set the bar at the highest level of integrity.

In my observation, individuals who gravitate towards the lowest or medium bar often seek a more convenient, though not necessarily easier, route. These lower-bar approaches are sometimes referred to as "levers." For instance, in financial reporting, some might find it acceptable to pull these "levers" to attain the desired earnings. In their perspective, without employing these levers, the company may struggle to achieve its objectives or face greater challenges in doing so.

There might be a reluctance among individuals to be perceived unfavorably by their supervisors, both direct and indirect. Perhaps they have made commitments or assurances to their supervisors regarding certain outcomes or directions, but when faced with the actual results—what I often refer to as "reality"—there could be a tension between those commitments and the present circumstances.

In specific situations, dynamics might involve one department extending support to another and expecting reciprocation, like Accounting favoring Financial Planning and Analysis (FP&A), so Accounting could provide leniency in accounting related policies and practices for favors from FP&A in flexible budgeting. This collaborative effort could be motivated by a shared goal of presenting a positive image to their mutual supervisor.

Consider pilots as an example. They rely on "reporting" to make several decisions. Pilots in the cockpit interpret real-time data from various instruments, forming the basis of their decisions. Pilots don't need to, and shouldn't, approach the engine while the plane is flying or walk on the wings to check things out. They depend on instruments and the data collected about them.

Imagine if flight attendants or engineers started adjusting sensors or metrics, saying, "Well, we're not that high up; let me tweak that sensor by X feet or this metric by this small amount." In such a scenario, pilots would be making decisions based on information that doesn't accurately reflect the reality of the situation.

There's a saying I adopted many years ago: "If you are faithful in little things, you will be faithful in large ones. But if you are dishonest in little things, you won't be honest with greater responsibilities."

The basic premise is that when people cheat in small things, then the chances of them being honest in big things becomes less. However, it's important to note that this doesn't imply people are either perfect or the worst. The point is that individuals, when conscientious in small responsibilities that earn trust, have the opportunity to succeed and be trusted with larger responsibilities over time.

Imagine a scenario where someone on the street hands you a dollar, asking you to pass it on to someone else. If there's no video evidence or tracking, and you decide to keep the dollar for yourself, it's unlikely you would have acted differently if entrusted with a larger sum. The principle here is that if you're not faithful with a small responsibility, it raises questions about your trustworthiness with greater responsibilities.

Choosing the "highest ethical standards" is crucial because it represents the best an organization can strive for. This choice avoids compromising on principles and emphasizes a complete commitment to integrity. While recognizing that perfection is unattainable and mistakes can happen, the Philosophy is to start with the highest standards, as accepting anything less might gradually normalize lower ethical expectations.

While many of the stories and examples provided below are related to accounting and finance, which is where I spent most of my career, all the principles apply to all aspects of the organization and one's personal life.

The Number's Game

On September 28, 1998, the Securities and Exchange Commission (SEC), the U.S. stock market regulators, delivered a speech titled "The Numbers Game." Within this speech, the SEC addressed various scenarios they labeled as "gimmicks." One particular aspect highlighted was the misuse of the concept of "materiality." The SEC questioned companies intentionally recording errors within a specified percentage ceiling, arguing that the impact on the bottom line is too small to matter. The SEC challenged this reasoning, questioning why companies would go to such lengths to create these errors if they were truly insignificant. This speech aligns with the highest ethical standard principles.

Interestingly enough, when the topics relate to accounting, finance or business processes, some in the business world express straightforwardly "these are not errors; they are an acceptable range of estimates." There exists abundant research, guidance, and regulations addressing how manipulating a range of estimates could be considered as "earnings management," which is generally disapproved of by regulatory bodies, especially when specific targets introduce bias into these estimates.

When a leader temporarily adjusts an accrual policy for just one quarterly metric to influence expenses, claiming it's immaterial when questioned, it prompts the SEC to question why such effort was invested if the matter is truly insignificant.

Mirembe's Story

Mirembe assumed temporary responsibility for a new function when the original leader, under the same supervisor, Joe, was reassigned to a different role. In addition to her existing responsibilities, Mirembe took charge of this function, including overseeing the books and records of the corporate ledger.

While reviewing the ledger, Mirembe encountered discrepancies and had a specific incident where she approached Joe to inquire about it. The discrepancies pertained to the timing and estimates involved in recording certain expenses and accruals.

When Mirembe raised the issue with her supervisor and later presented her perspective on why she deemed the accrual inappropriate, her supervisor inquired, "Do you believe what we are doing here is illegal?" Mirembe responded, "Legal or not, I will leave that to the attorneys. What I am asking here is whether it is ethical, and more specifically, if it could be considered the highest ethical standard when everyone is aware of the facts, including regulators, internal management, internal audit, or our external auditors?"

In Joe's perspective, he did not perceive his actions as "wrong" because they were not illegal, considering it fair game.

I had a similar experience while working with a service-based company. The company used time tracking, which primarily relies on a system where employees record or monitor their hours according to specific contracts or engagements.

Within time tracking processes, there was a practice known as "eating time," wherein some individuals could manipulate the process. In situations where the customer was billed a fixed fee for an engagement, spending more time would reduce the margin or profit rate. Some individuals engaged in "eating time" to artificially inflate the rate.

The root cause of "eating time" varied, ranging from individuals charging less time than spent on the project (because they try to appear more efficient hiding the actual hours worked), to supervisors wanting to meet specific metrics or expectations set by higher-level executives.

Refusing to engage in the practice of "eating time," I considered it comparable to lying or cheating. As I progressed in the company, I recognized that when reporting diverges from reality, regardless of the magnitude, decisions and conclusions drawn are not grounded in the actual situation or reality.

Unless the staff/senior reports time accurately, reflecting the reality of the situation, leaders might remain unaware of the true circumstances. It could be that the fee was insufficient or that there were changes on the client's end, justifying incremental fees. Perhaps the staff requires additional training or support. Reporting the time "as is" provides an honest reflection of the situation.

When individuals manipulate or "eat" time, the altered reality can lead to various issues. For instance, leaders relying on capacity schedules might assign more work based on inaccurate chargeable hours. This can create problems when additional tasks are added under the assumption of available capacity, which, in reality, may not exist. Honest reporting ensures that decisions are grounded in the actual circumstances, preventing unintended consequences.

Similarly, this concept applies to financial reporting, extending to various types of reporting, both financial and non-financial. Reflecting on the aforementioned incident with accruals, the question arises: When accruals are altered arbitrarily or expedient "levers" are employed, how does this impact the long-term understanding of the root cause? It conceals the fundamental issue at its core. Why was the forecast inaccurate? What factors contributed to deviations from the anticipated figures? This pattern often continues, raising further questions.

These levers become one-trick-ponies, diverting attention from the actual root cause of the problem. In a culture that heavily relies on these quick fixes, the organization becomes accustomed to opting for easy solutions simply because they are convenient.

An organization that embraces the highest ethical standards as a fundamental part of its Philosophy is more likely to achieve long-term success. This commitment ensures that issues related to Processes, People, or other aspects are not hidden, enabling effective problem-solving. Acknowledging and recognizing problems is the initial step in resolving them, as one cannot address an issue that remains unnoticed.

HIGHEST ETHICAL STANDARDS MODEL

If you adhere to this Philosophy, here is a straightforward model to follow when evaluating whether your actions, lack of action, decisions, or statements align with the highest ethical standards.

Here is the model:

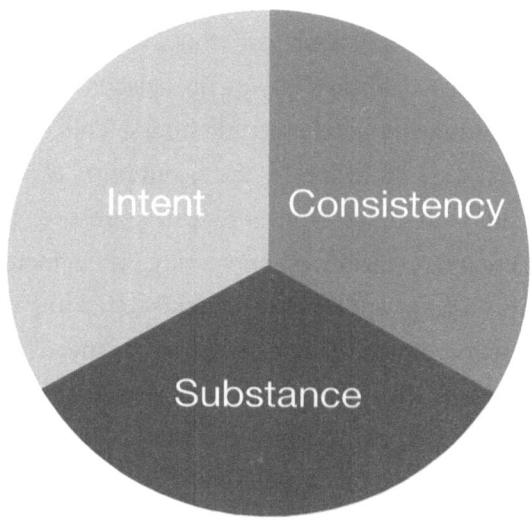

The three main categories of the Model are 1) Intent, 2) Consistency, and 3) Substance. These become the main categories to help you as a leader, or a follower, determine whether the decisions, actions, lack of actions, that you are making or have made would be considered as following the "highest ethical standards."

Let's break down these three categories and then discuss them collectively.

- **Intent:** Intent is indeed a critical aspect when evaluating actions and decisions. By asking "what is the intent here?" or understanding the purpose behind an action, it helps in assessing whether the motive aligns with ethical standards. In the context of the accruals stories shared above, it's evident that the intent was not driven by a genuine effort to improve accuracy or address an underlying issue. Instead, it was focused on achieving specific numerical targets for personal or organizational gain. Assessing intent provides clarity on the ethical foundation of an action.

    Intent can be masked or misrepresented, especially when

individuals or organizations attempt to justify their actions or lack thereof. In the case of Enron executives, it's plausible that they might have framed their decisions as being in the interest of shareholders or the broader society. This tactic is common when individuals want to create a narrative that aligns with positive intentions, even if their true motives may have been different. Evaluating actions against stated intent requires a critical examination of whether the proclaimed objectives genuinely serve the greater good or if they are merely a cover for ulterior motives.

By the way, "intent" is the only difference between fraud (with intent) and error (with no intent)!

- **Consistency:** The subsequent inquiry involves examining the organization's approach to comparable situations in the past. Are our actions and decisions aligned with the principles and methods we have previously employed in similar situations?

  Occasionally, altering the reporting or approach to a situation can be entirely acceptable, considering the presence of new information or evolving and continuously improved methodologies. However, it's crucial to question why there is a deviation from consistency. This brings us back to the underlying "intent" discussed earlier. The absence of consistency might raise concerns, depending on the specific facts and circumstances.

- **Substance:** This is a fundamental question. What is the "substance" of the transaction or event that is being assessed? When the event or transaction is financial, financial reporting at its core aims to portray the reality of transactions, financial condition, etc., through numbers (and sometimes footnotes). It is, to a significant extent, a translation—converting the actual financial health of an organization into a set of statements that incorporate numbers and footnotes. In accounting guidance, there is a principle known as "substance over form," which consistently guides accountants. This principle should also be applied to non-accounting and non-financial reporting matters. What is the substance of what you are trying to assess? It could be related to a legal case that you are trying to assess, or a business deal, negotiations with customers, communications and relationships among colleagues or family, or a policy setting in the public arena. No matter the topic or situation, looking at substance over the form of what is being assessed is crucial to determining if one is following the highest ethical standards.

The three factors mentioned above must be carefully considered in any situation. What is the intent? Are we consistent, or do we have a valid reason for any inconsistency? And, finally, what is the substance of the transaction or situation (also referred to as "reality")?

Additional considerations exist, but I view them as supplementary aspects to bear in mind rather than integral core questions. When utilized, sometimes these factors might turn into conscious or unconscious bias toward Intent, Consistency and Substance.

Materiality (or Significance) is a crucial concept, as highlighted in the SEC speech shared earlier. Applying the 80-20 rule can be beneficial, ensuring that organizational efforts are focused on significant matters, both qualitatively and quantitatively, rather than immaterial or insignificant ones.

Thinking in terms of risk is indeed valuable. Prioritizing efforts based on the level of risk, whether quantitatively or qualitatively assessed, ensures that significant matters receive the attention they deserve. While materiality plays a role in resource allocation, it cannot serve as a justification if the Intent, Consistency, or Substance of an action fall short of the highest ethical standards. Understanding why certain actions are taken becomes paramount in maintaining integrity and ethical practices.

If the facts in a given situation varied slightly, and the impact results in a different direction, would the previously deemed insignificant amount suddenly become significant, prompting a different course of action? Examining consistency in such situations helps uncover the underlying intentions behind the decision-making processes. Take an example of a trip to the grocery store and the cashier missing a charge for a certain insignificant item that you purchased. Would that prompt you to bring it to their attention? If you justify your action of not saying anything because the amount is insignificant, would you do the same in the inverse if the cashier charges you twice for the same insignificant item?

Detection Risk is the evaluation that influences the decision to take or avoid a particular course of action, often biased by the likelihood of someone detecting all the relevant facts and circumstances related to the item.

John Wooden's statement, "The true test of a man's character is what he does when no one is watching," emphasizes that an individual's genuine character is revealed when they act with the highest ethical standards, assuming transparency and accountability. This perspective suggests that a person who maintains integrity and consistency, regardless of whether they are observed, has nothing to hide and remains true to their principles in all situations.

Adam's Story

Adam encountered a situation involving a company's CFO that oversaw multiple segments and reported results at both the segment and sector levels (one level below the segment level). The structure included sector presidents, with each sector being accountable at its level. Monthly and quarterly meetings, along with reports, were organized based on sector-specific information.

During one quarter, Adam observed a change in the reporting structure of one segment led by the CFO, in collaboration with the VP of Investor Relations. Instead of following the usual sector-level reporting (horizontally by sector), they shifted to reporting "by type" of contract/customer (vertically). This change contradicted the company's operational structure and how segments were managed. According to regulations, financial results should be discussed in a manner consistent with the actual business operations. While others may have been unhappy with the change, Adam was the only one to raise the issue.

In a significant meeting attended by the CFO, various senior executives, legal representatives, segment presidents, CFOs, and other direct reports,

Adam chose to address the change in reporting structure when the discussion reached that section of the report.

Adam inquired during the meeting, expressing his curiosity about the change in reporting for segment X. He questioned what response the company would provide to the SEC if asked why the reporting format was altered, especially since it didn't align with the actual business operations.

Adam might have considered it a rookie mistake to ask the question in the meeting, but he felt compelled to do so as a last resort, given that no one else seemed to be addressing the change in the reporting format for segment X.

Despite the CFO's dissatisfaction with Adam's question, Adam clarified that he wasn't claiming the company was doing something wrong but was merely seeking to understand how they would respond if the SEC inquired about the change. The CFO's response suggested a dismissive attitude, asserting that the SEC wouldn't raise such questions.

The question of whether decisions and conclusions would have been different if everyone knew all the facts is crucial. It prompts reflection on the impact of transparency and full disclosure. Considering the hypothetical scenario of the facts being published on the front page of the Wall Street Journal encourages a reevaluation of actions in light of potential public scrutiny and accountability.

The described methodology is adaptable to every facet of an organization. It can be used when interacting with employees, suppliers, customers, regulators, and more. It prompts self-reflection, urging individuals to assess whether their conclusions, decisions, or actions (or lack thereof) are influenced by detection risk.

This framework extends beyond professional realms like accounting and financial reporting, serving as a valuable guide for decision-making in all aspects of life. The underlying principles remain universally applicable.

DIVERSITY, EQUITY, AND INCLUSION

The next category that organizations typically have as part of their core values is related to their employees. Typically, you will find a core value or a series of them relating to Diversity, Equity, and Inclusion (DEI). Originating in the US in the 1960s, DEI gained increased prominence in the early 2020s. It evokes diverse reactions, with some embracing and embodying its principles, while others, including governments, expressing aversion and attempting to prohibit its use. Let's spend some time assessing the term and then its effect on your Core Values and Philosophies.

Juan's Story

Juan's supervisor invited a guest speaker to present during a meeting of all direct reports, as well as participants from various departments. One of the speakers, Valentina, was a director from the HR department who was part of the team overseeing the company's DEI efforts. Juan, not being one of the speakers, attended the meeting to observe and be available for any questions. As Valentina began her presentation, she started going through her prepared slides.

In one of the slides, Valentina presented her organizational chart, placing herself at the top with about 6-8 team members below her. Notably, her title on the chart included "DEI," while everyone else's included "D&I" without the "E." The next slide contained various pieces of information, along with a formula:

$$D+I = ENGAGEMENT$$

"Engagement" serves as a measure of how "engaged" the employee workforce is in their job or position, which affects the organization's results (as discussed in Chapter 1). In the context of the HR presentation, "Engagement" is achieved through the reflection of both "D" (Diversity) and "I" (Inclusion) into the culture of the organization.

Juan pondered, if HR believes that D+I equal Engagement, what happened to "E" in "Equity?" And if Equity is not part of the equation, wouldn't that imply that E equals 0? If D+E+I is the same as D+I, then E really is 0, according to simple math.

This story made me think through the DEI Philosophy. Could Diversity and Inclusion be complete without Equity? Though I am not an HR professional, I am an expert in creating desired cultures. And since I do love analogies, I started thinking through the role of DEI from that perspective.

The Story of the 10 Microphones

Picture a team of 10 people, myself included, sitting around a table with microphones for discussion. If, upon observation, all 10 individuals resemble me in appearance, behavior, and thinking. A reasonable person might express concern due to the lack of diversity in thought or ideas, which could be detrimental to the company. To enhance "Diversity," the logical step would be to invite individuals to the table who do not share my appearance, behavior, or thinking.

Now, let's consider that changes are made resulting in Diversity at the table, but some individuals are not provided with microphones. In this scenario, even though you have achieved Diversity—there are individuals with varying characteristics at the table—true and substantive Diversity must encompass Inclusion. In this case, Inclusion would mean you provide microphones, allowing them to actively participate in the discussion. Inclusion ensures that everyone at the table has a voice in the conversation, and it ensures that Diversity is not only in form, but also in substance.

Yet, after providing microphones to everyone, you observe disparities in the volume of each person's voice reflected in discrepancies in the value assigned to them, such as compensation [when in the context of employee rewards]. In this case, you may have Diversity and Inclusion, but is the imbalance in volume reasonable? That's where Equity and Equality would come in. Let me clarify the difference between the two using the same analogy.

Equality would be achieved if, in the analogy, every individual in the room receives an equal seat cushion, regardless of their position or role—whether a CEO or a clerk. The focus is on providing the same benefit to everyone, emphasizing equal treatment without considering individual circumstances or contributions.

In the context of Equity, rather than Equality, it recognizes that individuals may have different roles, responsibilities, and contributions based on market conditions and principles of supply and demand in the context of professional occupation. While a CEO may receive higher compensation than a clerk, the key is to ensure that these differences are justified by factors such as contributions, market conditions, and experience (regularly referred to as "merit"). Equity seeks to eliminate disparities in compensation that arise due to factors other than merit and individual contributions.

Juan's consternation over the exclusion of Equity from the DEI model that Valentina presented was further exasperated when the company's first D&I report was published, and the title had no mention of Equity (E). The following year, Equity was included, resulting in the report being titled the DEI report. However, upon examining the report's content through a simple word count, Diversity (D) was discussed around 100 times, Inclusion (I) about 90 times, while Equity (E) was mentioned only around 20 times.

Further along in Juan's story, he attended a meeting with numerous participants from various functions. During the meeting, one of the executive engineers made a statement that seemed to imply, "Well, yes, we expect our company to have 50% females and 50% males, considering there are 50% of females in our world" (based on the equal chance of female-to-male birth ratio).

Juan observed a mindset that is based on 50:50 statistics. Although the rate is factual, he wondered if anyone had stopped to ask how many female engineers were available to recruit? How many exist locally in the market? Also, is the 50:50 ratio focused on the whole company? What happens if there simply aren't enough female engineers; would the company counteract with female non-engineers so that they have the equal ratio for the whole company? What happens if they do that, are they arriving at a computation of 75 males to 25 females engineers but for all other functions they must employ 25 males to 75 females? Even though they arrive at a total of 50:50, in reality are they discriminating against females in Engineering and against males in non-Engineering functions?

In reference to the above example, think of the Philosophy and how that influenced the culture. When Equity is based on anything other than merit, influencing task assignments, promotions, demotions, and compensation decisions, it will inevitably result in a divide at any organization and will cause lower employee engagement.

I was employed at a company when they hired a new CFO. She was very energetic and quickly produced a new slogan, derived from the company priorities which were "Grow, Innovate, and Perform." She focused on a line called "Performance First" which is the idea that unless we perform on our contracts with customers we will not grow and won't be able to innovate (regardless of which one comes first). However in her mind, rightfully may I say, unless the company performs first, it is unable to grow or innovate.

So I adopted a similar Philosophy for DEI, which I call "Performance ONLY." The reality in DEI is that unless all of it is wrapped in Performance ONLY, you will inevitably end with what the HR profession calls "reverse discrimination."

Martin Luther King Jr. said, "I have a dream that my four little children will one day live in a nation where they will not be judged by the color of their skin but by the content of their character."

The "content of the character" in the context of employment, work or career is no different than performance—it is something you achieve, choose and control. The content of character is what should be judged in a person because it is what they can control. Similarly, in the content of DEI, performance and merit is what should be judged in one's work, not anything else. Rewards should come based on performance ONLY.

If Diversity is the result or objective, Inclusion ensures that Diversity is in substance and not in form only. Then Equity ensures that the Diversity is well balanced and that it doesn't lead to the same phenomenon that it is trying to prevent.

DEI needs to be thoughtfully considered and measured, then, compared to a market for the purpose of ensuring there is no bias, explicit nor implicit, conscious, or unconscious. The core values of an organization must acknowledge the benefits of having a Diverse and Inclusive culture but also must ensure it is done with Equity and based on "performance-ONLY." As you think of your core values, remember that this is the "how" of achieving your Vision and Mission, and the Philosophies of how you treat your employees will have a significant effect on your culture.

COLLEAGUES NOT EMPLOYEES

The way you, as a leader, think of your employees [in other words the Philosophy you ascribe to] will dictate how you treat them and talk to/about them. This will be reflected as part of your core values.

I collaborated with a German-based company that was a very well-oiled machine. They closed their books every month by day 2, were ready to report by day 4, and were one of the first to report their annual reports on the DAXX (the German stock exchange).

I didn't know why at the time, and perhaps didn't even realize the full extent of it, but this company cared greatly about culture. It was embedded at the highest and all other levels of the organization.

I recently saw a social media post showing a letter to the company employees from the CEO and in it, I was very much surprised at the tone and specific language he used; even though I knew how favorable that company's culture was. In the letter, he doesn't address the employees as such, but rather, he addresses them as "Colleagues." Wow!

After seeing that, I went to their website and started surfing. I saw other messages from leaders that used the same term, "Colleagues." How amazing is this mindset? Imagine the revolutionary and positive impact it will have on any organization. Naturally, your "Employees", by law and on various formal documents, must still be referred to as such. But by choosing to refer to them as Colleagues, you elevate their status and value.

There are significant differences in how you, as a leader, interact with others when you see them as colleagues, rather than employees. If the CEO refers to her or his employees as Colleagues, then how do you think the remainder of the executives will treat them? This Philosophy will certainly create a close, respectful, and dedicated team.

This brings up a conversation that we will have in the next chapter on "walking the talk."

PERFECTION VS. EXCELLENCE VS. CONTINUOUS IMPROVEMENT

Typically, core values will include some notion of the quality of the organization's offerings that cover internal and external services.

I'm sure that most of us know the scene from one of the greatest movies of all time, "Remember the Titans." Coach Boone is at training camp with his team, the Titans, and says, "When you put that uniform on, that Titan uniform, you better come to work. We will be perfect in every aspect of the game. You drop a pass, you run a mile. You miss a blocking assignment, you run a mile. You fumble the football, and I will break my foot off in your John Brown hind parts...and then you will run a mile. Perfection! Let's go to work."

It seems like perfection is what we aim for—no mistakes. But if you look within the mindset of Coach Boone, even within the words that are used in the movie, you actually start to see a pattern and an expectation. "You drop," "you fumble," etc. There is an expectation of imperfection, not in terms of aiming for that, but rather, in a realistic probability of an outcome. You will drop a pass, you will fumble. But you will practice in order to not do either.

Coach Vince Lombardi once said, "Practice does not make perfect, perfect practice makes perfect." This is what Coach Boone was talking about—the reason you run a mile after a fumble is so that you don't fumble again. It's a continuous improvement mindset.

I joined a company as the lead on multiple sub-functions and my responsibilities were continually changing. I had Lombardi's phrase in mind and was upfront with all my teams. I always said, "I want to improve this" whatever "this" is. How do you tie the approach of continuous improvement with the notion of perfection?

Perfection at an organization will always be too costly. Look at the Pareto principle which states that for many outcomes, roughly 80% of consequences come from 20% of cause. It's the 80-20 rule. So the more you work on something to make it "perfect" the more costly it is. It's the law of diminishing returns.

So instead of aiming for perfection, aim for excellence. On the way to excellence, practice perfection, but never forget to continuously improve. While both perfection and excellence deal with the quality of the outcome, perfection leaves no room for imperfection or shortfalls, from a cost-benefit analysis.

If you keep a mindset of continuous improvement, that's when quality will increase at a faster rate than the passage of time. The same principles actually exist in the bestselling book, Atomic Habits. The whole premise of the book is that continuous, small changes over time translate to big results.

THE FACTS

In Plato's book "Republic" is the quote, "I'm trying to think. Don't confuse me with the facts." This is a statement or philosophy that is an irony; that what I think and what the facts are could be two different things.

An organization that is not principled on facts is gambling with their success and future. They might win every now and then, they might even get lucky at times, but eventually, they WILL lose.

Facts play an important role in organizations, but they don't operate on facts alone. There is a level of instinct and experience that must also be considered. The distinction here is clear, making decisions without a sufficient level of facts (quantitatively and qualitatively) is a formula for long-term loss.

While there is a sufficient level of facts that you need to draw on to make decisions, there is also the need to not over-analyze everything. "Analysis paralysis" is real and it's not good for an organization or a person's life.

When I practiced public accounting, there was a certain partner at the national level who set the guidance, the training, and the principles. He was very well known and spoke at many of the training workshops and national meetings I attended. I remember seeing and sometimes interacting with him during my first years at the company until he left many years later.

The man was deeply knowledgeable and very smart. There was one thing specifically that made him very well-known. His initial answer to questions—ANY and almost ALL questions—was "It depends." No matter the type of question, and no matter the details in the question, his answer, always, was "It depends." But after this initial answer, he would proceed to ask more questions and based on those questions he would give the answer.

Why did he do this? Facts and circumstances mattered highly to him. I remember initially that his "it depends" answer would drive me nuts. But as I matured as a professional, that model became one of my main Philosophies. I tried to balance the principle with the circumstances of the question, and many times, the person asking the question. But, unless I had a sufficient level of facts, I would give an answer of "it depends" and then add the principles of what the answer really depended on. This value ties directly with the highest ethical standard model discussed above.

THE NON-NEGOTIABLE

There is a lot that goes into running and leading any organization. There are goals, processes, employees, vendors, customers, regulators, etc. Leaders will be faced with tough decisions while they are moving the organization in the desired direction.

Throughout my career, I have faced tough decisions and witnessed countless leaders face the same. In many instances I would try to categorize the decision that needed to be made by classifying it as an "art" or a "science." It is a little harder to argue with science because in many instances science is factual. But when it comes to art, the decisions in this category are more subjective—they are not categorized as right or wrong.

On the other hand, I developed this principle that I call the "non-negotiable." When you deal with Philosophies embodied in core values, you should be in a different territory than when you deal with the details of processes or procedures. Philosophies should be much harder to deviate from while processes and preferences are the ones that you can negotiate.

What is non-negotiable to you when you consider the direction that your organization needs to take and how it will act on the way there? Asked another way, what is core to your organization's values? You can't make everything non-negotiable, but not everything can be negotiable either. This question will also help you differentiate between a value and a core value. Your list of core values should at least include what you would consider non-negotiable. I refer to it as your "irreducible core."

As an example, my five values that I consider non-negotiable are adhering to the highest ethical standard, striving for continuous improvement, respect, excellence, and recognizing that People are the heart of the organization. It doesn't matter how big or small the situation may be, if there is extra time or not, or if the budget is too small, etc. I consider these five values as my core values.

During the first Town Hall meeting with employees and the greatest CFO I have ever worked with, one of my colleagues stood up at the end and asked him a question that sounded like this: "As you know, we are going through a lot of changes in the company, do you have any thoughts or words of wisdom to people who say we just have too much work and can't get to all the things we want to do or accomplish? Without any hesitation, the CFO said "I don't buy that. We can never say we have no time for something. You know what needs to be done, you know your priorities and you know what needs to change. Yes, I agree, we don't have time to do everything we want to do, but that doesn't mean we stop there. Put it on a list and prioritize with the mindset that you are working through the list. To just say we have no time and move on is unacceptable to me."

This CFO understood the concepts of continuous improvement and the outcome this culture would bring to an organization! In fact, two of the CFO's non-negotiables were continuous improvement and highest ethical standards.

CONCLUSION

Philosophy (or mindset) is an important element in how you create the desired culture in an organization. While this could be easily overlooked or not even contemplated in organizations, it is the first step to achieving a desired culture.

In fact, it could also be the root cause of why your culture is what it is.

The next question is, how do you put all of this into a Process? Let's keep going!

QUESTIONS TO PONDER

1. What are the various Philosophies of the organization you lead or influence?

2. Do you have Vision and Mission statements? If yes, is your Vision statement time bound or is it endless? Is it focused on who you serve or self-focused? Is it inspirational to all people involved in your organization? Is your Mission statement the best steppingstone over the next 3-5 years to your desired vision?

3. What are your core values?

4. Is integrity one of your core values? If yes, do you differentiate it and aspire to the highest levels of integrity?

5. Do you have a process of assessing what you would consider the highest ethical behaviors in comparison to others?

6. Do you ascribe more or less value to any of your core values, or do you treat them all the same?

7. How do you think of your employees? What is your Philosophy about DEI? Do you consider your employees as Colleagues?

8. How do you think of the quality of your service, internal and external? Is it driven by perfection? Excellence? Continuous Improvement?

9. Do you have non-negotiables? What are they?

10. Are you a "facts-driven" organization? Do you make decisions exclusively based on feelings or significantly influenced by feelings?

CHAPTER FOUR
PROCESS

"Success is neither magical nor mysterious.
Success is the natural consequence of consistently
applying basic fundamentals"
—Jim Rohn

Once the Philosophies of an organization are defined, leaders must then embed them in what's called, Process. This becomes the path to instill these Philosophies in People, which then strategically results in the desired culture.

Towards the end of my tenure at KPMG, I worked with an insurance client. The lead partner, with whom I was extremely impressed, bought a book for all the team members entitled, "Above the Line," written by Urban Meyer, a famous college football coach.

I started reading the book, and not too far into the chapters, I found a nugget of information that crystallized something I have thought good and hard about for some time. But Meyer put it in such a way, that the pieces all came together for me, making a significant impact on my leadership style and later, on how to create and sustain culture.

He wrote, "Average leaders have quotes. Good leaders have a plan. Exceptional leaders have a system." If Philosophy is the quote, and strategy is the plan, then the "system" is the Process.

An organization might have a great Philosophy depicted in a great Vision, Mission, and Core Values statements. The leaders might even "walk the talk," have the highest ethical standards, and live and breathe a well-balanced DEI in their organizations. Yet, until they put all of that in the Process, or affect it through a "system," as Meyer's quote indicates, they will not accomplish the results of having People who are driven by the desired Philosophy.

That's why, in this chapter, we will discuss the need for a "system" —a Process that includes the importance of Principles, and Tools. In fact, the Process Principles are Philosophies that directly shape and define the Process. Process Tools, on the other hand, are a means to create and embed the Principles in the Process. As I cautioned you in chapter 3, there are many ways to embed your Philosophies in the Process. Following are ideas and principles that will serve as a good starting point.

PROCESS PRINCIPLES

Functional Equity

Every function in an organization is important and adds value, or at least it should. Some function aspects are direct customer facing, some are not. But at the end of the day, every function in an organization has a reason to exist; they all work together, serving each other in order to ultimately deliver services and/or products to the customer or stakeholder. So even functions that are considered non-core by some would still have a significant effect on others because every function has internal, or by extension, external customers. Problems arise when inequitable value or emphasis is placed on any one function.

Juliette's Story

During a company-wide meeting, Juliette's CEO was discussing some of the Company's strategies. One of these strategies was the centralization of some of the financial indirect functions and/or processes—things like payroll, vendor management, billing, collections, indirect taxes, fixed assets, and more. The CEO characterized these activities as "non-value-add."

Juliette started thinking through the statements. If the CEO thinks that these activities are non-value-add, is he saying that they add no value? Juliette knew that her CEO was a great leader and had accomplished what a million others couldn't. Yet, she just could not imagine being one of the employees who worked in Shared Services all day, being told that what they do "adds no value." How could a great leader not see that their work added value to the company?

Does the CEO actually think their work is not important? Maybe in his mind, he doesn't believe that Shared Services are core to the business itself because they are not a direct revenue generating function, but does that make them "no-value-add" to the company or its process? Imagine the effect of that statement on any employee in that function, let alone the leader of Shared Services who is charged with inspiring employees to give their all and do their best.

Even if the business core employees do what they are supposed to do, what happens if the process and activities related to Shared Services are not performed at the same level of excellence as the core or direct revenue generated processes? Would the organization continue to fire on all cylinders?

Juliette continued to ponder and ruminate over the situation. What happens when accounts payable doesn't add vendors correctly or pay them on time? What happens if indirect taxes are messed up or if accounts receivable mismatches the funds from customers? There was no doubt in her mind that if these systems were not in place, the core direct revenue generating employees could not function at their best, if at all.

When I think about Juliette's story, I recall many stories I have shared in this book. Remember the CEO of one of the companies that had a disproportionate value ascribed to HR? HR was a function that in this particular organization was disproportionately valued by the CEO, who is the leader of the enterprise. This negatively affected the culture of the company.

The reality is that all the functions of a company, business, or organization should not be categorized as more significant than another. All functions are part of the process that makes the organization succeed. It's similar to how the human body works. We often see the brain and the heart as the most significant parts of the body. However, our lungs and our kidneys are just as significant as well. Where would we be without our feet and our toes to help us to stand and balance? Think about the work that our hands do on a daily basis. Every part of our body—the seen and the unseen—work together to create the process of our physical life. No one part is insignificant in this process! I know one can live without a hand or a foot, but the point is that all parts come together to serve each other and provide the purpose they were made for.

In the same way, every function in a company has its purpose,—they are all important and add value because together they form the organization itself.

We also have to consider the discussion from Chapter 3 about Equity and Equality. Not all functions' budgets should be the same. The legal department budget has to be higher per person than the facilities department. One employee group finished law school and there are a lot less people that are qualified to perform legal related activities versus one who is ensuring your air-conditioning and heating system is working. It doesn't mean that the legal team is more important than the facilities team. Not at all. You will always have to make sure that every function is treated with Equity and ascribed the appropriate value; a wise leader would know that no one can function at their best when the air conditioning is not working, especially in Florida [where I live]!

The bottom line is that multiple factors should go into the allocation of resources to each function and person in an organization, but in the end, they all add value and should be treated with Equity.

The Story of Boeing

Boeing is another example when it comes to functional equity in relation to their culture and the Max 737 issues. When Boeing merged with McDonnell Douglas back in 1997, they had an "engineering-focused culture" while McDonnell Douglas had a "finance and cost-conscious culture" run by Finance.

Prior to the merger, Boeing was known for its engineering prowess and the delivery of the world's finest fleet of aircraft. So what happened? After the merger with McDonnell Douglas, a disproportionate weight was given to Finance while their once impeccable reputation for quality took a backseat. And sadly, these quality issues were hidden for years.

Remember the Vision statement of Boeing discussed in Chapter 3, which focused on being the largest in the aerospace industry? After years of a resultant culture, we find a disproportionate weight and value given to Finance vs. other functions, resulting in what we see today in the massive faulty design and quality issues of the 737 Max aircraft.

Finance in general must have a customer service mindset to both internal and external customers. So within an organization, Finance [at its core], is there to "shed the light" on where the organization wants to go. In other words, if the CEO and Chief Operating Officer choose the path, then finance's job is to "shed the light" on the path they choose.

Another function of Finance, which often lands in the CFO suite of responsibilities, are jobs that increase cash inflow or reduce cash outflow. These tasks include stewardship of cash/investments/assets to make sure the company is performing in the surplus and receiving their best return on assets as well as minimizing the tax liability of the organization. These services provide more resources to the organization at large to spend in critical areas like Research and Development, Engineering, and Quality Assurance.

Functional Equity is important because when an organization puts more (or less) emphasis than it should on any function including Finance, then this results in unbalanced or disproportionate value ascribed to this function.

When Finance is thought of as a "leader" that has more say than it should, the core Philosophy of shedding the light will be affected negatively. It's a case of the tail wagging the dog! If that happens, you probably will find situations that sacrifice quality of direct customer service and delivery because cost is elevated higher (and valued more) than quality.

However, in situations where finance is given less value than what it should have, it is equivalent to an organization running in the dark. So when the business or direct functions enter into contracts or arrangements without consulting their "light bearers," the accounting or other financial characteristics might not yield the best results if Finance was not involved prior to executing the contract with the customer.

The same can be applied to functions within functions. For example, functions within finance, depending on the size of the company, might include leaders in Accounting, Financial Planning and Analysis (FP&A), Taxes, Treasury, Internal Audit, etc. If the CFO puts more or disproportionate emphasis on one function vs. another, then you will have problems.

Giovanni's Story

Giovanni worked with an organization who had a CFO who "grew up" from the FP&A side of the house, and because of that, he always put more emphasis and ascribed more value to FP&A team members as compared to other Finance functions. In fact, most of the new projects went to FP&A individuals along with a greater proportion of executive promotions.

What kind of culture do you think that created? Certainly one that values FP&A more than Accounting or any other Finance function.

During a meeting at Giovanni's company that included Accounting, FP&A, Tax, and other leads, (along with their employees), the VP of Tax was asked about a certain invoice that came in prior to the end of the quarter from one of the consultants. She specifically said, "I am waiting on Jack (the lead of FP&A) to tell me what to do with the invoice; book it or not." Since this was a large public company, it had clear guidance on when [and what] to accrue regarding invoices that are pending from vendors, or when invoices are received. There was no reason to wait on Jack from FP&A for an answer since the accounting policy clearly states that the invoice should be expensed. But in Giovanni's company, FP&A was the most important function within finance, so Tax wasn't going to do anything with the invoice until Jack told them what to do.

If Finance at large "sheds the light," then each function within Finance plays a role in displaying that light. Accounting ensures that all transactions and balances are accounted for appropriately under the relative accounting principles and company policies. FP&A uses the historical data and the knowledge of the business to analyze the past and prepare for the future. Tax ensures that the tax obligations and all that come with it are appropriately booked, paid, and as much as possible, minimized in accordance with tax regulations.

Treasury ensures that the cash and investments/assets are maximized for better returns on investments/assets, and so forth. When one function is disproportionately valued, then problems start to arise. And instead of shedding the light, the whole process becomes a tangled maze of darkness.

On the surface, the FP&A function should be focused on analyzing and planning, to a point that they can predict what the final numbers should be. The problems start to arise when FP&A (or the CFO) puts more value on that function and starts to trust FP&A more than Accounting.

The same lessons apply to other functions and sub-functions within. If you categorize your HR organization between rewards, benefits, and compliance, do you ascribe more or less value to any one of them? Similarly in Operations, if you break that out to Facilities, Continuous Improvement, and Supply Chain, do you ascribe more or less value to any of them? It doesn't matter what the function is—all work together to achieve the vision of the organization.

Scott's Story

Scott worked with a large publicly traded company. During meetings with the company CFO, all Finance functions would have a seat at the table. The CFO would go around the table, one function and one person at a time, and ask them their opinion on the matter being discussed. The person could be a VP or staff, it didn't matter to the CFO. The CFO would never provide his opinion until others shared their views. This resulted in every function feeling equal treatment and a culture where everyone genuinely felt safe to express their true opinion. There was no "agreeing with the boss" culture because you didn't even know the boss' opinion!

At that organization, Finance was held in high regard, but it wasn't disproportionate to other functions. Similarly, within Finance, all functions were held with great esteem. Every function had its clear Vision and Mission of how they supported Finance and how Finance supported the other functions at large. When a new contract was contemplated, Finance would be brought in early in the process to "shed the light" on the accounting treatment and determine if there are ways to achieve the financial objectives without using any "levers" (as discussed in Chapter 3). At the time, the culture of that organization propelled it to be one of the most successful in its industry.

Functional equity increases organizational harmony, which significantly increases the chances of achieving the organization's objectives.

Repeatable Sustainable

A "Repeatable" Process is one that can be done again and again. It typically doesn't require customization or changes from one time to another. Think of it as something that can be consistently applied without much variation.

A "Sustainable" Process is one that can be maintained at a reasonable rate or level.

Actions or Processes might be repeatable but not sustainable, or, sustainable but not repeatable. An example of a repeatable Process is a superstar employee who is working 20-hour days for multiple days in a row. That person might be working efficiently, firing on all cylinders, but the problem is that their work in no way can be sustainable because that person will burn out, quit, or have health issues.

An example of sustainable but not repeatable is a group of employees that are on a team (or in a function), and all are working 8-hour days, which is very sustainable, however, they keep switching roles every hour or daily. By switching roles so frequently, they never have a chance to repeat the task frequently enough to make it more efficient.

Any organization would benefit from the principles of "repeatable sustainable" when affecting their Philosophies through a Process.

Efficiency and Effectiveness

As an organization affects its Processes by its Philosophies, it has to keep in mind whether these Processes are designed in the most efficient and effective way.

When changes are made to Processes, the end result must lead to more effectiveness, or more efficiency, or both. If it doesn't, then the organization should be thinking hard as to why they are implementing these changes.

Efficiency is based on quantity or value. For example, to make a Process more efficient, one might automate it through usage of a particular software.

I remember one year at my workplace; a group of employees went together (among many other people) to a Continued Professional Education (CPE) event at a nearby university. While I was sitting in the back during one of the sessions, an employee was sitting in front of me with their laptop open and doing work. I knew it was one of the employees from my company because of the logo in the background on the screen.

For an hour, this employee was typing and adding formulas into Excel. It was an hour-long exercise of enter, copy, paste, enter, copy, paste, enter, copy, paste, row after row. I must admit that I was going crazy watching this person labor through the redundant exercise. I kept on saying to myself there has to be a better way to do this. I know it wasn't a big deal, but I couldn't help wondering what else does this employee do that takes a lot more time than it should?

After finishing college, I temped at a large bank in the securities function. One of my jobs, which was also shared by another temporary worker, was data entry. So for hours at a time, I would take a certain sheet and, depending on the sheet and the type of security, I would enter specific data. After a few weeks, I noticed that the data being entered stayed the same based on the type of security and only changed when the security changed.

Eventually, I found a pattern and created a macro. My boss would give me a day's worth of work and I would finish it in less than an hour. I would take my work to him, and he would be surprised at how quickly I did the job, that is until I showed him what I was doing. Funny enough, because it was hourly work, I would sit there and do nothing for the remainder of the day. And my boss, who was a great boss by the way, didn't have anything else for me to do so I would be completely bored.

Effectiveness is the quality of the output, task, or Process. Let's say a task or a project was kicked off to reduce the company's tax rate. That is an effectiveness project because it will reduce the cash outflow of the organization.

There are some projects or tasks/Processes that deal with both Efficiency and Effectiveness at the same time. For example, sometimes the customer invoicing process is overly manual and as a result, takes too long to complete and is often rife with multiple mistakes which requires quite a bit of rework. By automating all or parts of that process, the organization can be efficient, because it takes less time, while also reducing the errors so there is no rework needed. The end result is that the customers are happy because the invoices are more accurate, which makes it more effective.

Remember, when engaging in a mindset or a Philosophy, it must be applied into a system or a Process where the organization will reap the most benefit by it being repeatable and sustainable, while also focusing on efficiency and/or effectiveness.

Efficiency/effectiveness and repeatable/sustainable can be argued as an actual mindset themselves, or at least a by-product of other mindsets or Philosophies. For example, if an organization has "stewardship" as a mindset and/or Philosophy, it will continually ask itself if the Process is the most efficient and/or effective that it can be. In turn, the organization would build and continuously improve Processes that are both repeatable and sustainable because they are stewards of the owners, shareholders or stakeholders' assets, and resources.

Automate, Offshore, Outsource

I learned the slogan "Automate, Offshore, Outsource" when I served a German-based company. I respected the company for many reasons, one of which was their culture of love and respect for the Process. This prioritization slogan was embedded in the company's Philosophy and Process. Without a doubt, every activity needed to be automated, period. There was no place for wasting time on manual processes. They MUST automate everything. Of course, this cannot always be done. In that case, they would then move to the next best thing and offshore it.

Offshore is the notion of moving the work, still internally for the company, to a lower cost location. Why pay someone $50 an hour to do a manual or not fully automated activity while you can do that far cheaper somewhere else? So they had multiple offshoring locations around the world depending on the task and center/skills of the offshoring location. An added bonus to this process is that when you send the work to someone else in the world at the end of your night, often that person you sent it to is just beginning their workday, meaning that when you come into work the next day everything is already done!

If for some reason offshoring is not economically viable, this company would find a sourcing company that does it for less and outsource the work to them. Whether it's offshoring or another outsourcing opportunity, why keep the work internally when you can have someone external do the work for less?

There is a term that is utilized in organizations called "scalable." This is the notion of being able to process or transact on a large "scale." In other words, taking care of a large quantity with little time or effort. Some utilize this term in conjunction with "repeatable and sustainable" by including "scalable" at the end of the slogan. The reason I didn't include it under the repeatable and sustainable discussion is because scale is relative to the size and resources of an organization. In my view, the scalable objective will eventually be achieved when an organization combines the principles of repeatable and sustainable with others like automation.

Counselors; not Consultants

An old proverb says, "For by wise guidance you can wage your war, and in abundance of counselors there is victory." Humility can be a difficult trait to possess, especially for confident, smart, and capable people!

Humility, as a tenant of Philosophy, is to acknowledge that there is no leader, no manager, no colleague, and no process or activity that is always (and will always be) perfect. In other words, there is always a need for advancement or improvement. Therefore, you will always need counselors or pre-established measures around you to guide you on your journey to achieving your vision.

I equate this need for guidance to a pilot. She has a co-pilot, a navigator, an air traffic controller in the tower, and all the flight instrumentation and data to assess the operation of the airplane and the course it's taking to get to its destination.

The idea of the above proverb is that while there is never a guarantee of victory in battle --yes, you should imagine your day-to-day life in any organization as a battle because processes break, and people change—the more counselors you have, the higher your chance of winning. The more minds that are looking at the problem, the greater the chance that someone will notice what another person has not.

So in an organization's collective processes and activities, there is always a need to have counselors, those who are invested in both the organization's and its People's success. These counselors should be willing and qualified and can be internal or external to the organization.

These individuals are best when they have the attitude or mindset of being counselors, not consultants. A counselor is invested in the Process and/or person to the point of a long-term, value-added relationship.

So what kind of a counselor do you look for? The counselor that you want on your journey, first and foremost, must have your best interest in mind. That means they invest in getting to know you and your organization—what you do, what Philosophy you adhere to, and understanding your measures of success. They care for your organization and are on board with the vision. In fact, a good counselor may even advise you to go with someone else because the other person or organization is a better option for you.

Counselors can be helpful in every aspect that we discuss in this book. Whether it's Culture, Philosophy, Process, People, or the various functions throughout the organization, choosing a Counselor that is invested in your organization is a highly recommended way to dissect an issue and find a winning solution. The frequency of calling on a counselor is dependent on internal and external facts and circumstances; typically, a 3–5-year refresh would be wise to adopt.

Collaboration vs. Consensus

Collaboration is a partnership or union of people that produce or make something together, while Consensus is the general agreement or unanimity of a group of people.

Though the line that differentiates between Collaboration and Consensus is very thin, the difference is stark. Collaboration is focused on the process while Consensus is focused on the outcome. The culture of an organization can be greatly affected by how it believes, promotes, and aims for Collaboration or Consensus, or even both.

Dale Carnegie wrote a book titled, "How to Win Friends and Influence People." In this well-known and revered book, Carnegie eloquently details multiple methods of making sure you will "win friends and influence people" as an end result. That can be achieved when others 1) naturally agree with you, 2) you agree with them, 3) you change their mind to your way of thinking, or 4) you gracefully disagree. At first, I thought the book was all about the outcome of winning friends and influencing people, which would mean achieving consensus. But once I finished reading the book, I realized that it was more about the process that will increase the likelihood of consensus but doesn't require it.

Another great book on the topic is titled, "How to Make Collaboration Work: Powerful Ways to Build Consensus, Solve Problems, and Make Decisions" by David Straus. It's interesting that within the title, the author interchanges the words collaboration and consensus. So once you build "consensus," you are then able to make decisions that solve problems which is "collaboration."

The book details great ways to achieve collaboration/consensus and provides ideas and processes of how to get there. In one of the chapters—when discussing What happens if you can't reach consensus?—there comes a point when collaboration and consensus clash. It acknowledges that consensus might not be reached and provides the solution of what Straus calls "the fallback option." He points to the process of defining who is the person accountable for the decision (See RACI Chart discussion under Process Tools below).

In another subparagraph immediately following the above, titled, "The benefits of having a fallback," Straus says, *"The existence of a viable fallback mechanism keeps people engaged in a collaborative process and helps to keep it shorter than it might otherwise be. It may sound counterintuitive, but if you acknowledge that consensus is not always possible, you increase the probability that it will occur. It's often the fear of reverting to the fallback that keeps stakeholders engaged in a consensus-building process. It's the fear of loss of control or the consequences of a win-lose process that keeps everyone engaged."*

The dangerous aspect of a "consensus first" principle or Philosophy, is that it might become the goal instead of the process. In Straus' writing, he articulates that the fear that some might have because of what the "fallback option" maker would do is what drives people to arrive at consensus. In my view, some might achieve consensus through an option or solution that might not be the best for the organization, which turns the consensus to the objective instead of the process. For example, you and your spouse are discussing where to go to dinner. You want Chinese food, and your spouse wants Mediterranean, so to avoid having someone else choose for you, you both compromise and reach consensus. You split the difference geographically and order Indian food, which neither of you like!

I know it is a silly analogy, but the main principle applies. Consensus might be achieved and aimed for, but it can't be the ultimate nor the first goal because the outcome might not align with the organization's or the group's objective and values.

Another aspect of Collaboration vs. Consensus that must be discussed is the notion of compromise. In the above example, the best outcome would be that one night the couple orders Chinese, then another night they order Mediterranean. That's compromise.

When you utilize the same principle in an organization, compromise becomes necessary but must be balanced within the Vision, Mission, and Values principles [along with others discussed above]. Is the group compromising on a Principle or simply a process? Is it a matter of personal preference or something deeper?

In Straus' book, while the title includes both consensus and collaboration, and though you always want to achieve consensus, can you achieve collaboration without consensus? The resounding answer is Yes!

When consensus mindset and resultant culture are strong in an organization, it results in everyone needing to sign off on everything. In these cases, "politics" enter in, and much time and effort are put into making everyone happy, especially the ones who are vocal. This mindset of incorporating everyone's opinion may dilute the effectiveness of potential solutions or courses of action.

Collaboration is the process, and one could argue that better decisions can only be achieved through collaboration. If consensus is always a must, even when there is a fallback option, decisions could be shaped to become the least resistant type and not necessarily the best decision for the organization on a long-term basis.

So ask yourself, do the principles that go to design your organization's Process center around collaboration or consensus?

Long-term vs. Short-term

In an effort to embed organizational Philosophies in its Processes, leaders will always face the difficult decisions between long-term vs. short term success.

A McKinsey study from 2017 found that the revenue of firms with a long-term mindset cumulatively grew on average 47% more than other firms, and their earnings grew 36% more.

There are many factors that drive leaders to ignore the above statistic. For one, the tenure of many leaders (take CEOs as an example) is less than long-term. In fact, the average CEO stays with an organization for 5 years and then moves on to another company. If their compensation is tied to the short or mid-term, why would they make a difficult choice that makes their organization less successful in the short term, even if it makes it more successful in the long-term?

Leaders who have the stewardship Philosophy front and center will care about the stakeholder at large, more than themselves. This is a by-product of the Highest Ethical Standards Philosophy.

I have often said, and will say it again, "Never sacrifice long-term success on the altar of short-term gains." Any organization that has this Principle as one of their core values, and embedded in its Processes, will always have a higher chance of success in the long-term.

Practice the Preaching

One of the most critical keys for an organization's Philosophy (mindset) to be efficiently, and effectively embedded within a Process (and followed by the organization as a whole), is that the leaders must practice what they preach.

I worked with a company who had extremely high ethical standards, but they had an incident that took place that serves as a good example regarding leaders "practicing what they preach." A company executive took an external stakeholder out for a meal to an establishment that one could characterize as not being 'family friendly' and charged the expense through to the company. When an internal auditor audited the executive's expense report, they took the name of the establishment and went online to see what it was about. The internal software tools blocked the website, which seemed odd at first to the internal audit team, but then as they investigated more, they found out that it was an establishment the company would not allow employees to go to for business purposes because it didn't agree with the company's family-friendly culture.

An investigation took place quickly and within a short period of time the executive was terminated. Though the executive did not adhere to the company's culture, the company itself had practiced what it preached without wavering. It was a non-negotiable to this company (as discussed in Chapter 3).

Contrast that story with another company who had a C-level quarterly financial review of a segment (where the corporate leaders go through the results with segment leaders). During the meeting, which I was listening to, the CEO noticed something that didn't make sense to him. He continued to ask and probe until the segment CFO confessed to something that was purposefully done against accounting policy; namely, expensing a capital improvement to boost profits that period.

The segment CFO continued to confess that he had directed his employees to override the accounting policy for a more favorable accounting outcome. The company CEO asked the CAO, "Is this right?" The CAO responded with a politically static answer, "It doesn't look right but I have to look into our policies." It was clear that the segment CFO knew it was a violation because he wanted to protect his employees, and said, "I directed my employees to do this." I knew that he knew it wasn't our policy, because if it were, the process would have been built to record it accordingly. Unlike the first company, this organization did not practice what they preach. The segment CFO maintained his job and was employed for several more years until retirement.

PROCESS TOOLS

Policies

Policies, written or spoken, become the main tool to affect and communicate the Philosophy that the organization believes. The larger the organization, the more written policies are needed. It is quite easy for a small business to communicate their Philosophy verbally and also through example (walk the talk). But when you have an organization that is larger, far more written policies will be required.

Policies can be arranged by topic and may be assigned by functions. Example of policies could include Ethics, HR, Accounting, Legal, Finance, Environmental, Health, Safety, etc.

The best policies are the ones in which leaders make clear connection to the Philosophies including the core values.

Trainings and Handbooks

Trainings are live or recorded sessions that are intended to reflect how the policies should be applied. They can range from very detailed, to high-level, to overviews. Depending on the size and composition of the organization, the trainings can also be high-tech or simple on-the-job trainings.

Handbooks, on the other hand, are utilized differently than trainings because they document the process of applying the policies or strategies and can be accessed on-demand. These resources can include code of conduct manuals or any others like it.

Many organizations do not spend as much time as needed to train their leaders. Although not the subject of this book directly, embedding into the Process a Principle that you value your leaders and want them to continuously improve would naturally focus on internal leadership trainings. Some would either ignore the topic or simply change leaders in hopes for better leaders although training the leaders will likely be much cheaper. The cost of replacing an employee can range from 30% to 150% of their annual compensation. Unless the issue is a disagreement with values or violations of policies etc., training your leaders will always be more effective and efficient than hiring new ones.

Annual Certifications

In order to confirm an acknowledgement by employees (and other stakeholders like vendors), organizations should utilize an annual certification process that encompasses all the key Philosophies and resultant policies. Many organizations include ethics and code of conduct as part of their annual certifications. These certifications can also target external constituencies like suppliers, customers, analysts, etc.

RACI Chart

When applying the Philosophies or the Process Principles in a Process, and depending on the size of the organization, leaders will have to define who is doing what and when.

In an organization that has a small number of people, a mechanism might not be as important because the breakout of roles and responsibilities will end up with one or two people doing everything. However, it is still good to keep the following principles in mind because you shouldn't have "too many cooks in the kitchen." In fact, the RACI Chart is designed to ensure that doesn't happen, as well as leaving no tasks or activities unassigned. I remember the first time I learned the term RACI; my eyes were immediately opened to a mindset/principle/Philosophy that significantly enhances the repeatable and sustainable aspect of any Process. It also embeds in a Process a certain Philosophy of accountability and responsibility that would come with rewards (or lack thereof when goals are not achieved).

You can easily find more information about this methodology online, but I will give an overview here because it is essential to our discussion about organizational culture.

The RACI Chart is a methodology that differentiates employees (People) by process, task, or activity between Responsible, Accountable, Consulted, and Informed (RACI).

Responsible

In this category, these are the people (or person) who are responsible for a process, task, or activity. They have been assigned the task to either start, advance and/or complete it. They are the "it" people when it comes to action. Like a soldier in battle, they are the ones who will take the order and make it happen. This could have more than one person assigned because one task might be given to two or more people to complete. The less the people per task the clearer the responsibility will be. If you are on a project and you have 100 people assigned to one task, you might want to break it down to lower-level tasks unless the task is the same for all 100 people. For example, 100 people will take 10 flyers and put them on dorm room doors throughout campus. If you don't care about the specifics of which dorm, and you just want the 100 to walk around and plaster the campus with the flyers, then there is no need to break the activity down.

Accountable

If you as a person or a function are accountable for a task, then you are accountable for the results and achieving the goal. This is typically the person who is authorized to make decisions, because one can't be accountable if they are not also authorized for decision making. Typically, there should only be one person or one function that is accountable, not more. Otherwise, there will be confusion as to who is making the ultimate decisions.

Consulted

This person or persons are consulted (notwithstanding the conversation above about the difference between Counselors and Consultants) by the Accountable person—who goes to them for consulting and expects feedback. They might be a committee, next level executives, or owners/shareholders who oversee the project but approve or veto based on a macro view of how the project affects a larger project or goal. These individuals approve what is going on at a higher level but are not the ones who are Accountable for the ultimate achievement of the specific project's goals.

Informed

In this category, the person or persons assigned this task are informed about what is happening. It is like a For Your Information (FYI)—you send them an email with status updates, but you don't expect them to come back with approval or advice (they could but that is not the expectation because that is not their role). These people are simply informed for awareness, for ensuring there is no clash with other projects, etc.

Another principle, which we will discuss in more detail in Chapter 5, is the notion of Rewards. Clearly differentiating roles and responsibilities must ultimately be connected with the rewards that the employee is receiving. Otherwise, employee engagement will suffer. Employees deserving more as a result of their high performance, but not being rewarded accordingly, will either be disengaged or ultimately leave the organization for a better or more equitable opportunity.

Organizational Structure

Depending on the nature of the business and its Philosophies, the structure of the organization needs to take into consideration the company's goals and the culture it is trying to achieve.

Typically, in a for-profit organization, you have the CEO at the top followed by the C-suite level leaders, including Chiefs of Finance, Legal, HR, and Operations (which depending on the size of the company, could include business operations in addition to other operations that are not direct to customers).

Some industries require more C-suite or a different composition of C-suite executives. For example, in the insurance industry, given the importance of investments, you might have a Chief Investment Officer, who typically in non-insurance or non-banking industries might be a VP under the CFO.

Organizational structure is affected by how the leader and/or other leaders apply the RACI Chart methodologies. This is also important when changes take place either internally and/or externally in an organization. In a company where responsibilities or accountability is not clear, tasks or functions could get lost or sometimes have multiple leaders. So depending on the culture, at best, these situations will result in inefficiencies and/or ineffectiveness.

I collaborated with a company which experienced significant expansion over a short period. It was noticeably clear that segments had autonomy to make their own decisions. But they were also going through a lot of centralization, since the culture of the company was moving from a holding company to an operating company.

The company had a Chief Information Technology (IT) Officer who would typically have authority over anything IT related. However, given the expansion of "data" in general, all sorts of "data-lakes" started popping up around the company. A "data lake" is a centralized repository that allows for the storage of large volumes of structured, semi-structured, and unstructured data in its native format, without the need for prior processing or modeling. Unlike traditional data warehouses, which require data to be structured and formatted before storage, a data lake retains data in its raw form until it is needed for analysis or processing.

It honestly became a nightmare. Duplication of efforts was taking place; consultants were being hired by both the segments and by corporate. It quickly became apparent to me that what they were doing needed to be changed, the sooner, the better. I quickly approached one of the VPs under the Chief IT Officer.

We spoke about the apparent inefficiency and confusion that was noticeably taking place at the company. He quickly told me that he was reorganizing his team and would hire a data-centric person. But the bigger issue was that this person was never given full authority or accountability over Data in general. The company was missing the designation of a Chief Data Officer (CDO).

This title or designation became a very important position at many organizations because the line of who owns the data between departments was starting to get blurred. Do the operating functions own their data? Does IT own the data that resides in the IT system? Can businesses create their own set of data that is not filtered through IT people? Is there duplication of efforts? Is the data secure, accurate, and complete to be able to make decisions? Are non-IT people even capable of making these decisions without IT?

All these questions are typically asked and accounted for by the CDO. So the confusion of the RACI Chart when it comes to Data (as an example topic) resulted in more money spent than needed and multiple duplication of efforts that could have been eliminated if the CEO and other leaders followed the RACI tool.

Measurable

To assess the achievement of any goals, they have to obviously be measurable. However, unlike quantifiable financial measures or non-financial measures, culture is a hard topic to quantify. After all, how do you measure respect? Teamwork? Thinking and acting at the highest ethical values?

Here are a few steps that simplify the process of measuring your culture.

What are you measuring?

The first step in measuring your culture is understanding what your organizational culture is made of and/or what do you desire it to be made of. What are the collective values that make up your organizational culture? Or what are the sub-cultures that you are trying to measure?

Evidence of what is being measured

The second step is to ascribe characterization related to these culture traits that you defined above (either current or future). For example, if one aspect of the culture you want to achieve is highest ethical standards, you pause and ask yourself, what does that mean? Maybe it means that you have high scores on employee surveys related to ethics? Perhaps it means that you buy all your employees ethics related books to read every year.

There are two ways to measure culture or sub-cultures after you define which ones you desire. I call them the input method and the output method.

Let's start with output, which is the measure of results. Think of quantitative measures like sales, headcount, or new customers. You then develop these measures based on your goals and on the culture characteristics that would help you achieve your goals.

For example, if you are trying to build a customer-centric organization that resulted from a desired culture of "customer first" Philosophy or core value, you would then develop customer-centric goals. One of your first goals would be pure numbers from sales. In theory, the more satisfied customers you have, the more sales, right? However, depending on the facts of the organization and its industry, what if you have more sales, but the sales per customer are less? Or, you are getting more customers that year, but it is due to a one-time special offering, etc. So when you measure the customer goal related to sales, you might also want to measure it as sales per customer.

Another way to measure the satisfaction of customers would be to ask them! As an example, many companies and organizations use customer satisfaction surveys. Based on the customer's satisfaction level, you can then measure an output (the results) if the customer is satisfied or whether they feel valued at the highest level. Once the survey results come back, then you can ascertain what type of culture your customers are perceiving. So for the output methods, you are focusing on the end results or its by-products.

Then there is the input method. Unlike the output method, this method focuses on the upstream measures that result in the desired culture or sub-cultures. The input method would focus on measuring the level that the organization believes is needed to achieve a certain culture trait. Then, the organization can reverse engineer that needed level and ascribe it to certain parts of processes that could be quantified.

Let's look at the customer-centric culture at a restaurant. First, define what constitutes customer satisfaction, which could be measured through customer surveys and targeted satisfaction goals. Then link the desired satisfaction results to the reasons why your customers were satisfied. If a restaurant believes that in order for a customer to be satisfied at the highest level, there has to be a certain welcoming atmosphere, then this atmosphere can be quantified and achieved when a certain percentage of employees are greeters. This way, when the company connects their employee targets with their desired quantified outcome (or output), they can then measure if they are meeting the input goals. By design, this will result in a good culture, that typically is measured through the output method.

I think of differentiating between the input method and the output method in the same manner as the relationship of the cause and effect. The input method is what causes the results. The output method is the results.

The reason organizations should also focus on the input method is because that would be proactive (input) vs. reactive (output) under Newton's third law (action and resultant reaction). So if an organization wants to be proactive, then they would initially start with the input method, then the results of the output method would be expected (although sometimes the reaction hoped for doesn't necessarily follow the action as planned).

This would also increase the likelihood of when the inputs, which go to affecting the output, are starting to fall behind the desired levels, the organization can get a head-start on discovering it and fixing the issues before they start to have an effect on the output.

Another aspect of measuring the culture is ensuring that all stakeholders are included in the process. I have been at many organizations where there is a disconnect between what the leaders see and believe vs. the on-the-ground personnel.

Root Cause Analysis

One aspect of measuring the culture or sub-cultures, including measuring the processes or certain activities within these, is the root cause analysis. This refers to how far back upstream an organization would have to go to change or fix issues. This is an especially important piece in the process that would determine whether changes will have the long-term desired effect.

Here is an example in the financial reporting arena. The company is a public company, and as required by US regulations, must have a process for employees to anonymously report ethics violations. Depending on the goals of the organization and the specifics of the reports, the organization might be looking at the results and focusing narrowly on processes but not taking a step back and trying to ascertain if there is a Philosophy issue.

Let's say the CFO of the above company believes that immaterial earnings management is acceptable and desired. He may even call it "levers" or "creative accounting. Let's assume at its core, just for demonstration sake, that immaterial earnings management is not considered a "highest ethical standard." If an employee calls the anonymous hotline to report it, then the "fix" that is only focused on the process, is temporary. That's because the root cause of the issue, which is the CFO's belief that it is acceptable, is not addressed. It will only be a matter of time before something is overridden in the processes, or the CFO changes the process to revert to an acceptable Philosophy of "immaterial earnings management."

This is also true when there is a favorable desired culture. Let's say the reason your culture is favorable and is the desired one is mainly because of specific people in the room or some key players in your organization. What will happen when these people leave or rotate out? Is your organizational culture the way it is because of "select" people or is it embedded so deeply in all aspects of your company that it would take significant influence of certain people in addition to a long period of time to change it?

Let's say the culture is so strong in the arena of the highest ethical standards, which came as a result of related Philosophies deeply embedded in Processes and trained very well in People. Even when a "bad apple" is added at the top executive level, this bad apple won't have the immediate negative impact because of how strong the culture is. However, if the bad apple remains, it will only be a matter of time before it leads to the deterioration of the culture.

The measuring of culture, when successful, will help leaders cultivate the culture or sub-culture. But for lasting effects, the organization must include analysis of root cause when unfavorable and/or undesired results are present [and sometimes even favorable results]. Then, the organization needs to carefully consider whether there is a link to Philosophies. If the organization focuses the root cause analysis on only the Process, that might mask that something needs to change with Philosophy. Alternatively, if the organization digs into the root cause through People, Process, and Philosophy, there will be a lot less risk that history will repeat itself.

CONCLUSION

After Philosophy is defined at an organization, putting it into a Process is no easy task. This is one aspect that differentiates exceptional leaders from average ones.

The next question is, how do you instill that Process in your People? We are getting close to creating the culture you want!

QUESTIONS TO PONDER

How do you currently embed your Philosophies in your Processes?

Process Principles

1. Do you appropriately value all the functions under your authority and treat them with the right level of functional equity?

2. Are your current processes repeatable and sustainable?

3. Do you have a mindset that ensures changes are either enhancing the effectiveness and/or efficiencies in your current process?

4. Have you adopted the philosophy of Automate, Offshore, Outsource?

5. Do you have internal and/or external counselors to help challenge you and your organization to cultivate a desired culture within your business?

6. What culture do your teams operate in? Collaboration or consensus?

7. Can your culture and/or aspects of it be characterized as short-term or long-term driven?

8. Do you and other influential leaders in your organization walk the talk? Do you practice your Philosophies and beliefs?

Process Tools

1. Do you have policies that clearly match your Philosophies?

2. Do you have trainings and handbooks, or other tools, that help you train your employees to achieve the desired culture? Do these trainings include leadership specific training?

3. Do you utilize annual or recurring certifications to ensure your employees understand your Philosophies?

4. Do you utilize the RACI Chart or similar tools to ensure clarity in your organization of who is responsible vs. accountable vs. consulted vs. informed on all aspects of the organization?

5. Is your organizational structure clearly designed to achieve the desired culture?

6. Do you have measures that you utilize to assess the maturity of your culture traits?

7. Do you spend a sufficient amount of time assessing the root cause of your current culture traits? Do you stop at Process, or do you dig deeper when there is an indication that it might be a Philosophy issue?

CHAPTER FIVE
PEOPLE

*"Coming together is a beginning,
staying together is progress, and
working together is success"*
—Henry Ford

Let me start this chapter with defining and differentiating People within an organization specifically in relation to the topic of organizational culture.

There are three kinds of People in any organization, Leaders, Followers and Follower Leaders.

Leaders are the ones that set and/or have a significant influence on the Philosophies, or the mindset. They are the sponsor, authorized, or Accountable (RACI Chart as discussed in Chapter 4) person to lead an organization, or parts of it like a function, process, etc.

Followers are the ones that follow the Process or Processes, while Follower Leaders are the People that perform both, Leading and Following, but do not lead the whole organization, function, or sub-group, etc.

Sometimes the percentage of Following vs. Leading could differ depending on the size of the organization. A CEO (or President) of a company is a Leader who is the ultimate Leader—the head of the organization. Though they don't Follow anyone, they are Accountable to the Board of Directors or Shareholders. The CEO is the one Accountable for the organization at large under the RACI Chart. Therefore, their Philosophies are integrated in a Process and instilled in People. So while there is influence by certain stakeholders on the CEO, the CEO is the ultimate person Accountable for their organizational culture.

Followers are People who perform the daily/ongoing tasks as designed by a Process. Though they might not have much influence on the Process, they are the ones who work with it on a day-to-day basis. While their experience with the Process—whether good or bad—can be helpful to the Leader, Followers are not the ones Accountable for the design nor the effectiveness/efficiency of the Process. Followers could include Account Payable clerks, Account Receivable clerks, HR staff, engineers, IT personnel, customer service, etc.

Follower Leaders could range from people reporting to CEOs such as CFOs, head of IT departments, VP of HR, etc., all the way to line managers, and people who lead Followers. The higher the Follower Leader is, the more authority they possess.

CFOs as an example, depending on the size of the organization, follow the CEO, so they are Followers of the ultimate Leader, nevertheless they will have a significant influence on the People in their sub-organization because they set the specific functional Philosophies to align (or sometimes not to align) with the organizational Philosophies.

The chief intention of this chapter is to cover the general mass of People in an organization, the Followers. They are the ones that will be the outward manifestation of your inward-beliefs, as instilled in the Process they are following.

PEOPLE, THE HEART OF YOUR ORGANIZATION

Spoiler Alert! In his book, *The Heart of Business*, Hubert Joly eloquently charts out the answer to the question "what is the core or the heart of a business?" with the clear answer of "People."

He details his experience and wisdom in how to "unleash the human magic." His book emphasizes that People are the heart of business, which is absolutely true. Without People you can't have an organization. I suppose one day the components of organizations will change, especially with Artificial Intelligence (AI) and robots. But ultimately, People will remain the heart of the business because you will always, at least for the near future, need People to design the AI and the robots. So Joly says that through People, you will achieve your results.

This book charts a different path but ends with the same results. People are the outcome of the Philosophy and the Process, since the Philosophy affects the Process, and the Process is followed by the People.

Following this path includes defining People as the Followers, not the Leaders. This chapter mostly deals with the Followers because previous chapters dealt with the Leaders.

It is the Leader (or Follower Leaders) who affect and adopt the Philosophy. It is the CEO of an organization or the head of any other organization (family, not-for-profit, etc.) who has, or should have, the Accountability and authority to affect and shape Philosophy. Then depending on the organization, either the same head or one or more layers below will have the passed-down Accountability (and Authority) to affect or shape the Philosophy in their function or lower-level processes.

Let's take accounting policy, which clearly is the reflection of a certain Philosophy. If you have a company that has a Philosophy of following the accepted accounting principles in a more conservative way, then the policies will take that Philosophy and put it in a Process through policies and practices.

The CAO or the CFO, again depending on the size of the organization, would have an effect or influence on the Process but it will always be the CEO (and the CFO for public companies) who signs off on the financial results of the organization as a whole.

While the CEO will have the Authority and specifically the Accountability to communicate the Philosophy, it is up to the CFO and/or the CAO to put that in policies and processes, or practice for People to follow.

Believing that People are the heart of your organization will propel you as the Leader to ensure that you take care of what keeps you alive! The remainder of the chapter will focus on ideas, processes, principles that help you instill the Philosophies into your People through the Processes as discussed in the previous chapter.

GOALS

Any organization, or any person for that matter, should set goals that are carefully thought through, documented, and tracked. There are certainly different ways and methods to set the goals, which are typically followed by many organizations. These goals could be different from one organization to another and even within the organization.

The following are some helpful goal setting principles/methodologies.

Directional Driven

There are two types of goal setting methodologies that are utilized by any organization, "top-down" and "bottom-up."

- **Top-down:** These are the types of goals that are set for the whole organization. Then, depending on the size of the organization, these may be broken down into different departments or functions within the organization. These goals can be scientifically driven (i.e. based on tangible factors) or might be more of an art (based on feelings).

    For example, top-down goals might be influenced by macro factors. In the commercial airline industry, the leaders might set financial goals based on the projected growth of commercial airlines traffic in the next period (a year, 5 years, 10 years, etc.). Or they could create a more "feels right" type of goal that says "increase sales by 3%" that are not based on industry specific projections but rather on their collective feelings.

- **Bottom-up:** Based on different factors, and/or, the facts and circumstances that are existent within a process, an organization can set their ultimate overall goal through a bottom-up approach. So the goal is set at the lowest or lower level, then compiled to arrive at the organizational level. Take any industry that functions through sales channels; the organization could reach out to every salesperson and have them set the goal, then compile it to arrive at the overall goal for the organization.

Culture Driven

There are two types of goal setting methodologies that are utilized by any organization based on their correlation to culture, "Typical" and "Culture- Focus."

- **Typical goals:** Organizations always have built-in goals like sales, profit, and other financial measures. In my view, these are the easier goals to set and track because they are easily measurable (as discussed in Chapter 4).
- **Culture-Focus goals:** Many organizations do not utilize these goals because they are harder to develop and track. These are the goals that directly or indirectly correlate with the desired culture.

    If a business is desiring a certain culture related to how their People should treat their customers, based on the metric they utilize, they would translate that resulting culture into a measurable metric. Then, in order to reflect it through People, they must ask how that metric would be satisfied. Considering the example from Chapter 4, a restaurant that decided to have a welcoming customer atmosphere could reflect that culture through a metric of the number of times greeters smile per customer. Once targeted at let's say 10 smiles per customer, then they would ask themselves how to instill that in their greeters.

    Another example would be an organization who wants a culture of innovation. They would set a goal regarding a number of new inventions (as an output method), or hours spent on innovation (as an input method).

If you want your organization and People to be driven by your desired culture, then you must elevate your goal setting process to also include goals that correlate with the culture you desire. These goals must also be pushed down to all People in the organization.

TRAINING

Vince Lombardi, considered by many to be the greatest football coach in American history, said "We win our games in practice. We learn and follow the fundamentals of our game better than anyone in the league. All of our games are won in practice." Interestingly enough, in the Arabic language, translation of the words "training" and "practice" are actually interchangeable!

When I specialized in public accounting, it was no surprise that our organization spent a great deal of resources on annual and ad hoc trainings. They knew that People, in this instance, their non-partner employees—from Interns all the way to Directors (the level before Partner)—are the heart of their business. So, they invested time and money training their People because they were the ones delivering the services to their customers.

People were their greatest commodity.

There was tremendous growth in the non-partner employees that resulted from the training sessions. In fact, I saw these results firsthand, not only because I was a participant in these sessions year after year, but also because I taught the training sessions for about 8 years. The firm was so invested in their People that they made sure their "trainers" were taught by outside "professional trainers."

I find it unfortunate that many organizations don't facilitate any kind of employee training, and those that implement some forms of training, only do it for certain employees—often the ones that are considered "direct to customers" (i.e. the money makers). Just as unfortunate, far too many companies do not include Culture in their training.

Just as in creating goals to achieve the desired culture, training sessions must focus on culture. I saw a video recently about the "In-N-Out" University—yes, they have a university where all employees go for training prior to starting their position with In-N-Out. I haven't had the pleasure to witness their live training sessions, but I wouldn't be surprised if they discussed direct and indirect topics that are culture related and would have a significant impact on their desired culture.

Training is essential to all People in an organization, not just the Followers.

When I interviewed for a CFO position, the head of HR asked me a question that stumped me. He said, "What leadership book are you currently reading?" At that time in my life I was not actively reading business or leadership books. I told him, "The main input for my leadership growth comes from LinkedIn and other types of articles." I never got a call back!

Though I didn't understand why he asked me that question, it was a revolutionary moment in my career when I realized that a good Leader is one who seeks out continual growth and improvement in their leadership skills and abilities. If a Leader believes they are perfect [or has nothing to learn or improve on] then they shouldn't be a Leader (or Follower Leader). Those who are good Leaders and want to be great Leaders know that they need to keep learning and improving each step of the way.

The answer regarding growth and improvement must always include training. Whether it's professional continuing education, leadership training classes and conferences, reading books on leadership and business, or joining a professional leadership group, there are many avenues to continue to grow and learn as a Leader.

So, from that interview point and on, I made it a goal for myself [and my teams at work] to read one leadership book per year. I would buy it for them, which was something that one of my previous leaders did, and it positively helped me in my growth as a Leader.

MENTORING

Mentoring is a positive process where a seasoned professional (a mentor) comes alongside someone (a mentee) who is in an earlier stage of their career in order to teach and guide them in their role at the organization.

I can't overemphasize the importance of mentorship, which is something that is agreed upon by many Corporate and Organizational leaders. It's not only important to the mentee but has many benefits to the mentor as well. Mentorship is a great commodity to the organization as a whole.

Mentorship adds a personal touch to the process of the organization's investment in their People. The mentor shares their experience and wisdom with the mentee. The mentor needs to be someone who is not the direct supervisor of the mentee (unless it is a small organization and there are very few people). Any organization would benefit from an official mentorship program or process.

REWARDS

As discussed in Chapter 3, performance should be the ONLY basis for any employee reward. Such rewards can include salary increases, variable compensation, commission, discretionary compensation, stock compensation, promotions, etc.

These rewards must be sufficiently differentiated between employees based on performance. I have worked for organizations that, no matter what the goal or performance level of the employee, made sure that the entire work force received a 2-3% annual raise, regardless of the employee's performance. Even if a high performer received a 3% increase, the average employee received a 2% increase. The differentiator wasn't meaningful to the one who had a better performance. In the end, this created a culture that disconnected rewards from performance and drove down employee morale. The effect was an overall feeling of employees not caring to excel.

There are benefits that should not be affected by nor connected to a performance differentiator. For example, medical insurance. An excelling employee shouldn't be rewarded differently from an average employee when it comes to medical insurance.

CHAMPIONS

There are multiple levels of what I call "Champions" at an organization, depending on its size. Executive Leaders who set the tone in the organization are all 100% Champions of the company's Philosophy, Process, and People, all of which when strategically aligned will lead to your desired culture. They are either a Leader or Follower Leader. Without them, there is no chance of creating or sustaining a desired culture. They are the ones that should "talk the talk" and "walk the talk."

Champion Executive Leaders must have slogans and statements of wisdom that communicate and embody the desired culture. They start meetings with culture statements, end meetings with culture statements, and have mugs and T-shirts depicting the desired culture. Remember Jeff Bezos and the "customer chair?"

In order for an organization to have a better chance of creating a desired culture in a maximized effective and efficient way, you will need Champions at the Follower level. These are the people whose official job title might not include the culture trait they are championing. They are similar to volunteers who believe in the trait. But, at the same time, they need to be rewarded for their effort and performance, and as time passes, they also need to have the culture trait or topic they are Championing as an official part of their scope.

At one of the organizations that I worked for, we wanted to significantly increase our function's buy-in and create a certain mature culture related to the same topic. We created Champions of that topic at each location. The level of accomplishment typically corresponded with the degree of buy-in from leadership. For the ones who were on board with the culture change, magic started taking place. These Champions became our ambassadors. They bought into the culture we were trying to create and as a result, they had a significant impact on their businesses/divisions. They were so excited that they were using YouTube on their own time to research the topic they were Championing. They were able to cut costs, increase effectiveness, and were empowered to make changes because they believed in what they were doing and received authorization by their Leaders.

BEST INTEREST AND CELEBRATING SUCCESS

I had a supervisor who was very bright and exceptional in just about everything. If it was politics, current events, accounting, they knew it all. That person was one of the youngest at their firm to make Partner. The person would give many great comments and also "nit-pick" comments on everything. Everything needed to be perfect. The person would review a document, give comments on it, then after fixing what was needed, they would give additional comments on their comments. Though exceptional, that person was brutal.

Despite the possibility of gaining a significant amount of knowledge from the experience, few people were eager to work for them.

Contrast that person with another supervisor who was almost as picky but wasn't as exceptional in the quality of their work. I loved working for that person! What is the difference? It came down to two things:

First, I knew that the second leader had my best interest at heart. When that person gave me more work or corrected my mistakes, it was always with the notion of "growing" my career. Yes, that person wanted my work to elevate to a better quality but, they also communicated with me in such a way to teach and make me a better performer.

Second, that person always celebrated success. Whether it was a lunch, dinner, or "end of engagement" events, they celebrated our hard work.

In order for the desired culture to thrive, Followers (People) must believe their Leaders have this type of interest in them and celebrate their success.

HIRE SLOW AND FIRE FAST

Unless an organizational culture is so sufficiently strong, to the point that nothing will affect it (I don't think that there is or will ever be such an organization), hiring and termination strategies, along with all the steps in between, must include an emphasis and prioritization of culture.

A fairly known slogan or HR Philosophy is, "Hire Slow and Fire Fast." Personally, while I agree with the main premise of this statement, I don't think expedience or haphazardness is the intention.

Since employees are the "heart of the organization," you don't want to just plug numbers or empty slots. So, the Hire Slow side is not intended to say that if you have an option of hiring the right person in a day vs. 10 days, you should pick 10 days because you must "Hire Slow." Rather, it is intended to say that good employees, those who will be a positive impact on the organization and have the right cultural fit (or at least will be easily moldable to it), can't just come by chance and can't be assessed for cultural fit that quickly or that easily. You must look for them, attract them, and make sure they are the right fit, either as a Follower or Follower Leader, and all of that simply takes time.

The moral of the story is "don't rush into decisions just because you need to fill a gap." Conventional wisdom and countless studies tell us that hiring the wrong person is a lot more costly than leaving the position open and hiring temporary employees until you find the right fit.

Please keep in mind that depending on the position, there is typically not a "perfect" fit. Don't keep it open because you are trying to hire a unicorn that doesn't exist. Instead, the idea is that hiring the right culturally fit person will always require thoughtful consideration and due process, which typically takes time. Hence the "Slow Hiring" slogan.

Firing someone is never easy. Reasons for termination may include that they are no longer needed at that position or at the organization as a whole, or the cultural fit is so off that it's having a significant negative effect on the employee performance and/or others around them. Whatever the reason for someone to be terminated, it needs to be a justified termination that is based on being fair to the employee as well as going through all necessary steps for legal requirements. Once the decision has been made to terminate an employee, it needs to be done in a relatively short amount of time (i.e. "fast"). The longer you keep the employee, the more damage that employee can cause within the organization.

When I took over a department, I came to realize that two employees out of about 20 were performing very poorly. Their work was slow and had poor quality. The person I replaced had been trying to deal with the situation for multiple quarters and HR didn't want to make a move because of the employees' minority status—creating a difficult and slow process.

So, when I took over and was assessing the team, these two were quickly identified as having an unfavorable effect on the team at large. In other words, they were bringing down the whole department. Their presence was terribly negative to others around them. After I tried to understand the root cause of their issues and then took a few weeks to figure out what could be done to fix it, we came quickly to the realization that it was time for them to move on. One of them had lied on their resume and simply didn't have the right experience for the job, and the other disliked the state we were in and wanted to move away.

As I worked with HR and presented the case—and it helped that I had a new HR representative who believed that the DEI parameters we had should not bias the employment action decisions—I was able to terminate these two employees very quickly. I held a meeting with the team afterwards to make sure they understood that there were no mass layoffs, and in a short time it became apparent that harmony was restored to the team.

CONCLUSION

After your desired Philosophy is strategically embedded into a Process that is then instilled in People, the three are strategically aligned, and you will have your desired culture! The above pointers, principles and ideas are only a small glimpse of what is needed to instill your Philosophies and Processes into People, but it is a great start.

Now that you have the desired culture, it's time to learn how to sustain it.

QUESTIONS TO PONDER:

1. Who are the Followers Leader and Followers in your organization?

2. Do you believe that People are the heart of your organization?

3. Do you set measurable goals to your People?

4. Do these goals tie to your desired culture?

5. Do you have different types of goals? i.e. not just the standard ones.

6. Do you spend time, money, and effort on training your People to follow the Process and to reflect the desired Culture?

7. Do you have a Mentorship program at your organization? Are you a mentor? Are you a mentee?

8. Do your Rewards programs follow your goals and desired culture?

9. Do you have Culture Champions at your organization?

10. Are you the type of Leader or Follower Leader that puts the employees' best interests at heart and also celebrates success regularly and when warranted?

CHAPTER SIX
SUSTAINMENT

*"Success is not final; failure is not fatal:
It is the courage to continue that counts"*
—Winston Churchill

John Wooden, the famous American basketball coach and player, said this about learning: "The eight laws of learning are explanation, demonstration, imitation, repetition, repetition, repetition, repetition, repetition."

Typically, creating something and sustaining it are two different animals. Yet the interesting thing about culture is that it's like planting or cultivating; there is almost no difference in the process between creating and sustaining. You need water, soil, and light when you plant the seed in the ground. While the seed buds and grows, you need water, soil, and light to bring it to maturity. And finally, when it is a large tree that bears fruit, you need water, soil, and light to sustain it. Just like John Wooden said above, what is needed to sustain your desired culture? Repetition, repetition, repetition, repetition.

Now, there are always some fluctuating differences when it comes to sustainment, but what worked well for you when you were on the path of creating your desired culture will be the very elements that help you sustain it!

Here are some ideas, processes, and principles that you should be thinking through in order to sustain the culture that has been built or is being built right now (remember, it is an ongoing exercise).

ARE WE ON THE RIGHT TRACK?

Humility is one of the most powerful traits a leader can have. It makes them recognize and acknowledge their imperfections, which cultivates an ongoing process of not only improving their leadership skills, but also their processes within the organization. All of this increases the chances of achieving their organization's goals, which align with their Vision, Mission, and Core Values.

The Leader and Follower Leaders in their organization must continually ask themselves, "Are we on the right track?" What is the best way to determine this? Although there are many ways to find the answer, I found that one of the most direct and honest methods to know whether the Leaders are on the right track is by surveying the employee groups, (best if anonymous), as to the culture of the organization. Another indicator besides anonymous employee feedback is the measurement of achievement and success within the functions a Leader has been assigned.

An important note, as a Leader, do not solely rely on feelings or beliefs for measurements because they can be deceptive and mislead you during the process of sustainment.

Another key to staying on the right track is to make sure you have a long-term history in building culture—it helps illuminate whether you are on the right track or not. Don't be hasty in your endeavors towards sustainment. Cultivating culture is a long-term exercise.

WHAT FRUIT DO YOU SEE?

Culture creation and sustainment is similar to cultivating a garden or crops on a farm. In all cases, as we just discussed above, the processes for creating and sustaining require the same essentials. And one reaps what they sow. One of the best ways of sustaining your desired culture is by looking at the fruit that has grown from it. Are your sales flourishing, or are they suffering despite doing what you think you should do strategically? Is there a section or a function of the organization that is having trouble no matter what you do? Are the processes you have in place effective and efficient, or are processes simply not working as they should? Are your employees or participants at large engaged in their day-to-day activities at your organization?

Remember the process of cultivating and planting. Are you doing the steps you are supposed to do but the fruit is not showing up? Or is it showing up but it's not in the quantity and/or the quality you desire? [See the output method discussed in Chapter 4].

WHAT'S THE MISSING INGREDIENT?

There are many elements that we have talked about in this book. The discussions about Philosophy, Process, People, and more were magnified with many examples, stories and analogies. But there is one ingredient missing from the equation that has been given to you in this book. You have all the information you need to chart your course and cultivate the seed of a desired culture at your organization. Yet, unlike the Philosophies, Processes and People along with other key details we have discussed, there is something you can't achieve, grow, or control.

When you plant a seed and expect it to grow and bear fruit, typically, you prepare, you plant, you nurture, you reap, right? Well, no, not really. Here is a better depiction of what really happens: You prepare, you plant, you nurture, and you wait... and you wait some more... and you are still waiting... extra waiting ... and you wait once more... and then finally, you reap. Culture, like plants, takes TIME to grow. But it's worth the wait.

Time is one of the greatest elements of culture creation and sustainment, yet also the hardest to control. It is the only resource that is given equally to everyone—we all have 24-hour days. If you are the Leader (CEO or President) or the temporary employee, you both have the same amount of time per day to utilize. One of the biggest issues that Leaders have is the seeming inequity between their workload and the amount of time they have to get it done. Do you know the feeling? I'm quite sure you do!

Maybe you can relate to the following story.

A farmer went out to cut the grass with his machete. The first thing he needed to do was to sit down and sharpen the blade. While he focused on what he was doing, a storm was forming and could be seen on the horizon. As the farmer continued to sharpen the blade of his machete, the storm was slowly continuing to approach. Neighbors and farm hands started screaming at the farmer, "What are you doing? Can't you see the storm is coming? Get up, start cutting the grass!"

Since the farmer was an expert in his trade, he knew that if he cut the grass with a dull machete, it would take him a lot longer to get the job done. But if he spent time sharpening the blade of the machete first, he would be able to cut the grass much faster. The farmer knew that getting the machete ready before cutting the grass was a wise investment of time.

It's the same way with cultivating culture. Spending time identifying, creating, strengthening, and sustaining your organizational culture is a wise investment of time that will alleviate problems down the road, and increase the chances of achieving your organizational objectives.

Skipping activities that effect culture creation and sustainment to "save time" will reduce the chances of achieving the success you are desiring. Take the time to cultivate culture. In the end, it will always be worth it.

WHAT'S NEXT?

Now you have it, the Secret Recipe. You now know how to create and sustain a desired culture. What's next? I suggest the following: think, collaborate, assess, plan, implement, and celebrate. Here are some thoughts to help you in your next steps.

Think

As articulated in this book, thinking or Philosophy is the first step to creating the culture you desire. What do you believe in your heart? Are you convinced about the positive results of culture and that you will be able to Champion this endeavor? Are you humble enough to walk this path? Is this worth it for you?

If you are not the ultimate Leader, are you willing to walk this path? What will the cost be? How far are other Leaders' thoughts, beliefs, and Philosophies from yours, especially the ultimate Leader? Are you willing to put in the time, effort, and political capital to create the desired culture? Initially, you can focus on parts of the desired culture—the parts that you can control, or the functions over which you are the Leader. Then, once you have the desired culture and the proof that it works, take that up the chain to convince the ultimate Leader.

If none of the above is possible, ask yourself whether your belief is strong enough or this book has opened your eyes to the root causes of why you are dissatisfied or not as engaged in your organization as you want to be. Maybe the culture is the reason, leading you to think about whether you are in the right organization. If you decide to move to a different organization, will culture be a focus during your interview process? At least you will go into it with your eyes open and can immediately work to cultivate a desired culture. In fact, your beliefs related to culture cultivation could become a selling point for the new organization! Who wouldn't want to hire a leader who is passionate about organizational culture!

Collaborate

If you are the ultimate Leader, collaborate about this topic and the contents of the book with other Follower Leaders who report to you. Remember, without them, you will not be able to integrate your Philosophy into the Process.

If you are not the ultimate Leader, talk to your direct reports and other peers. Share with them the book and any other resources that can convince them to join your endeavor. Maybe wait until you are able to affect the culture you desire in your sphere of influence and let the results speak for themselves!

Either way, always remember that collaboration will be more successful when anchored in Philosophy. Therefore, keep the Vision, Mission, and Core Values discussion up front and center in all you do. The "why" will always ignite the passion of Followers.

Assess

Assess your organizational culture at the top level but also within. We have included an assessment tool at the end of this chapter to help you with this exercise. Focus on the Model and on the skills of your Leaders, including your own skills, if you are the ultimate Leader. Is your model strong? Separately, are your Leaders strong? Are you and they a "Leader worth following?" Are you willing to enhance your leadership skills?

Remember, while this book's intention is to help you cultivate your desired organizational culture in a systematic and process-driven way, having good Leaders will significantly increase your chances of success. These are two sides of the same coin. As you complete the assessment, ensure that you are focused on differentiating the results between the Leaders and the Model. This will help you with the plan because the implementation for each is different. Remember the analogy of the race car driver? The plan to improve the driver is significantly different from improving the process that supports the driver.

Depending on the size of your organization, you might have to do this exercise by function. Start with one function to test this out then expand to others once you have the desired results. Alternatively, you can start with one or two topics instead of a wholesale approach to one function. For example, given how important the Highest Ethical Standards core value is and its pervasive effect on any organization, you should assess that aspect first.

If you don't know how to assess or have no time, don't let that stop you. There are plenty of resources that you can utilize that won't cost much and will have a good return on your investment. Find an expert "counselor" who can help you complete the assessment. Always remember that this is a long-term endeavor. If you include culture in your goals, I am almost certain you will achieve it!

Plan

"If you fail to plan, you plan to fail!" Put a plan together and remember that it will take time. Break it out into chunks. In golf, for a putt that is longer than 15-20 feet or 4-6 meters, the golfer will start to visualize the putt based on different sections. That increases the chance of a successful putt. The same goes for you. Break this out into different sections over a longer period of time. Make sure to collaborate and include others in this plan.

If you are a small organization, with fewer than 50 employees, this endeavor will not take long to achieve; my guess is about 3-6 months. I've talked to many smaller organizations and the typical answer is "we love this, but we don't have time." Try to focus on what can you reduce from your current load in order to replace it with the culture creation activity. Keep reminding yourself and your team about the story of the farmer, shared above. This book, some online courses; and culture-centric Q&A webinars would be sufficient to get you on the right track.

If you are a mid-size organization with fewer than 250 employees, this endeavor might take you about a year to achieve and will probably require some level of outside "counselor" help in addition to this book and some online courses.

If you are a large organization, over 250 employees, and especially when you have over 1,000 employees, this could take you up to 3 years. If you are a large organization, 10,000 and more, it will take an estimated 3-5 years. Any large organization will have sufficient resources to invest in this topic. In addition to reading this book, you should also have an internal leadership academy to ensure you cultivate a culture of strong Leaders that are worth following. You probably have an executive or group of executives that are Accountable for continuous improvement. Add culture to their list.

No matter the size of your organization, utilize the RACI Chart (or similar tools if you are a small organization) to assign tasks that are specifically related to the desired culture creation. Utilize SMART goals—Specific, Measurable, Attainable, Relevant and Time-based.

Implement and Celebrate

Once you have a plan, start to implement the SMART actions. Compare your implementation to your plan on a frequent basis; no less frequent than quarterly. Don't forget to celebrate each step of the way, especially if this endeavor will take you more than 3 months. Celebrate in chunks, by time phase, by function, and by topic. Find ways to celebrate because implementing and affecting organizational culture is worth it!

It is my deepest desire that this book and many other resources that we offer will help all of you create and sustain your desired organizational culture for the ultimate good of humanity.

QUESTIONS TO PONDER

1. How often do you ask yourself and the other Leaders in your organization whether you are on the right track or not?

2. Do you see the fruit of the culture you desire in all aspects of your organization?

3. Do you spend enough time on culture assessment, creation, strength, and sustainment?

4. Do you have a plan to apply what's in this book? Have you shared it with anyone else?

5. Are you celebrating your successes with your organization?

EYAD J. MUBAIED

ASSESSMENT OF YOUR ORGANIZATION

What is the maturity of your organizational culture? The following Assessment will help you determine the answer to that question. To access or download an electronic version of the below assessment, please visit:

http://www.cultivateculturellc.com/cultureassessmentcdo

(Follow the instructions provided)

ORGANIZATIONAL CULTURE ASSESSMENT

The objective of this assessment is to determine the maturity level of your organizational culture.
Complete the below questions for your organization. Some functions might have different maturity; feel free to average the functions to arrive at an overall score for the organization.
Your answers should reflect the reality of what the average employee feels.
Average all the answers, the higher the rating the better your culture is. Individual or average answers less than a 4 will require a deeper dive.

	Less		Moderate		More
Philosophies	1	2	3	4	5
• How well is your vision statement defined and communicated?					
• How well is your mission statement defined and communicated?					
• How well are your core values defined and communicated?					
• How well do you feel the organization's stated values align with its actual practices and behaviors?					
• How well do you feel the organization values the highest ethics and integrity?					
• How important are teamwork and collaboration within the organization?					
• How balanced is the organization's values around Diversity, Equity and Inclusion (DEI)? (5 rating if balanced)					
• How would you rate the effectiveness of leadership in promoting a positive work culture?					
• Do you feel that leaders within the organization embody the values they promote? Do they walk the talk?					
• Do your employees feel that the leaders have a servant leadership (5 rating) attitude towards them?					
• Do your employees feel that the leaders prioritize the long-term (5 rating) prospects of the organization vs. the short-term ones? (1 rating)					
• Do your employees or workforce feel comfortable (5 rating) providing feedback to your managers and colleagues?					
• How transparent (5 rating) do you perceive the organization to be in its communication with employees?					
• How receptive do you believe the organization is to new ideas and innovation?					
Process					
• How well do you think the organization adapts to change and embraces new technologies or approaches?					
• How balanced is the value provided for each function within the organization?					
• How repeatable and sustainable are your processes?					
• How efficient and effective are your processes?					
• Do you feel that your processes within the organization embody the core values? Do they align?					
• Do you feel that the organization clearly differentiates roles and responsibilities using the RACI chart methodology?					
• Do you feel that the organization structure aligns and enables the achievement of the vision, mission and core values?					
• Do you feel that the organization measures success and connects the measures to vision, mission and core values?					
• Do you feel that the organization digs deep when assessing the root cause of issues? Do they fix issues at the surface or does the organization take action to ensure fixes are permanent?					
• How effective do you find communication channels within the organization for sharing information and feedback?					
People					
• How engaged do you think your employee or workforce is?					
• How satisfied are your employees or workforce with the opportunities for professional growth and development provided by the organization?					
• Do your employees or workforce feel valued and appreciated for their contributions to the organization?					
• To what extent do your employees and workforce feel empowered to take risks and make decisions?					
• How likely are you to recommend the organization as a great place to work to others?					
• How satisfied are you with the work-life balance provided by the organization?					
• How linked are your rewards (salary, bonuses, etc.) with performance only?					
• How well do your people communicate with each other? Is there "drama in the office", unnecessary conflict, inefficiency and dropping the ball?					
• How well are relationships among your employees? Is there gossip, turfwars, mistrust, or toxic environment? (Less rating if answer is yes)					
• How well is alignment among your employees? Is there wasted efforts, lost time, duplicate work, or division?					
• How well is the execution of your employees at large? Are there unmet goals, blown budgets, missed deadlines, or damaged credibility?					
• How is your employees capacity? Are they burned out? Are there missed opportunities, high turnover, or stagnation?					

MEET THE AUTHOR

Eyad J. Mubaied has more than 24 years of experience as a leader in Corporate America and has served some of the most distinguished organizations. His background spans finance, leadership, and culture transformation. Eyad is an author, business owner, consultant, and coach who inspires leaders and organizations to cultivate their desired culture. He has a B.A. in Accounting and is a CPA. Eyad's certifications include GiANT® Coaching, Five Voices, Altitude, and Intensives. He has helped and nurtured various organizations in diverse industries, both locally and globally.

Through his company, Cultivate Culture LLC, Eyad is a noted speaker and Coach. He also conducts workshops and webinars for corporate, non-profits, mid-level, and small businesses.

Eyad has been married for 23 years to his beautiful wife, Christie, and has three teenagers, two boys and one girl, who inspire him each and every day.

His passion for organizational culture led him to write The Culture Driven Organization book, in which he shares his experiences and the Culture Creation Model.

MEET THE COMPANY
CULTIVATE CULTURE LLC

Cultivate Culture LLC, started by Eyad J. Mubaied, is driven by a vision to cultivate every organization's culture for the good of humanity.

At Cultivate Culture LLC, we believe culture creation and sustainment is achieved through two sides of the same coin: Leadership and a Culture Creation Model. Both are vital for shaping your desired culture. That's why we focus on two key priorities:

- Leadership: Our GiANT® leadership services aim to enhance leadership skills at all levels of the organization.
- Culture Creation Model: Our Culture Creation Model services are inspired by The Culture Driven Organization book to assist organizations in creating their desired culture through their Philosophy, Process, and People.

At Cultivate Culture LLC, our services include assessments, courses, workshops, coaching, webinars, keynote speaking, and the Culture Driven Organization book.

We exist to serve leaders and their organizations, big or small, for the good of humanity.

info@cultivatecullurellc.com
www.cultivatecullurellc.com